Politics for Pa

Politics for Partners

How to live with a Politician

Alicia Collinson

With cartoons by Hoby
www.hobycartoons.com

Politico's Media

First published in Great Britain 2007
by Politico's Media
PO BOX 279, Tunbridge Wells, Kent, TN2 4WJ

A catalogue record for this book is available from the British Library.

ISBN10: 1904734197
ISBN13: 9781904734197

Printed and bound in Great Britain by Biddles
Cartoons by Hoby, www.hobycartoons.com
Designed by John Schwartz, john@thefrontline.net

Contents

More than 'Two for the price of one'

Sometimes it's enjoyable and satisfying being the spouse or partner of a parliamentary politician. At other times, it's pretty tough and lonely. Looking back at the life and talking with other spouses and partners, we felt we'd mostly been left to discover how the system worked for ourselves: every one of us individually reinventing the wheel. We thought a book of advice and ideas, with strategies for common problems, might be really useful for newcomers right from the start of the selection process. "Politics for Partners" is the result of these discussions. Not a wholly original idea, since it draws from an earlier pamphlet "Two for the Price of One", written in the 1980s. That excellent work was only distributed to spouses after the politician had been elected, though – probably too late to make a real difference.

Acknowledgements

This book has been compiled with the unstinting assistance of numerous current and former wives, husbands, children and partners of current and former politicians – some elected, some not – as well as many of the politicians themselves. It's by Conservatives, for Conservatives: although some aspects may have wider relevance. To all those people: grateful thanks. Apologies are owed, as well – some of the language is infelicitous, since it attempts the tall order of being neutral about gender, marital status and sexual orientation.

> ❝ I've lost count of the number of times I said 'Hear, hear!' while reading ❞

Initial points

Start as you mean to go on

Everyone advises you: "Start as you mean to go on". They explain that if, in your new role as the politician's spouse or partner, you immediately go to every event; back every cause; and get involved in every campaign: you may experience huge problems if your commitments change. That's excellent advice, but how do you gauge the right level of involvement from the start? And how do you then manage the very significant transition after election, from the single focus on the constituency to the dual focus of a life split between Westminster and the constituency?

Make your own choices

There's no single right or wrong way to carry out the supporting role. Don't believe anyone who says you must do something in a particular way, if it doesn't seem right for you or your family or your career. The person you're talking to may well have had a completely different experience of political life. Even if they are your predecessor in the same constituency, they are very likely to be at a further stage of life. So: be yourself. You'll probably be criticised by someone – whatever you do – so you might as well feel comfortable and in control of your chosen course. Don't cram yourself uncomfortably into other peoples' expectations.

Relationship problems are not included in 'Politics for Partners'

This book does not set out to give guidance on relationship problems. That would take up an entire, separate, book. You will need to work out with your politician, for yourselves, how you live your personal lives. While political relationships are probably no more likely than others to become controversial or to break down, it does happen. Keep in mind that if things go wrong, 'personal' seldom equates to 'private'. It often seems the Press believes the Public is voraciously fascinated by the tangles of politicians' private lives, however obscure the people involved may be. Don't be surprised if you find yourself the subject of media attention purely for that reason.

Skip what you already know or don't need just now

'Politics for Partners' is primarily intended for newcomers to political life, and goes into specifics which may be glaringly obvious to more experienced readers. Some of the issues listed may only arise in a few constituencies and not in yours; or only at specific times.

'Politics for Partners' isn't meant to depress you

For reasons of space, this book concentrates on the pitfalls you might face, and leaves you to discover the fun for yourself: so please don't be discouraged if you find it a catalogue of woe. If you know problems might arise, you can probably avoid them or get over them sooner, and get on with enjoying the treats, thrills and fun of your supporting role. In addition, there is a great deal of material in this book which will only apply after your politician becomes an MP – but if you're setting out on that road you need to have a reasonable idea where it's leading you and what's to come.

> 66 The only chapter missing was how to ensure each day contains 26 hours instead of the standard 24 99

Starting out
the selection process

> ❝ There aren't many jobs which change your life overnight. Being an MP's spouse/partner is one of them ❞

Be ready for the long haul

Few politicians are selected by the first seat to which they apply. Most appear before numerous selection meetings until, seemingly at random, a constituency association selects them as candidate. It's a bit of a lottery, depending on many factors over which you have little control. Don't take it personally. Try not to become too keen about any one seat – with or without family connections – with or without the perfect house – since you're statistically likely to be disappointed. Remember, too, that past results, and past boundaries, do not guarantee success or failure at the next election or beyond.

Express your interest in applications early

It is likely you will have scant involvement in the process of applying for parliamentary constituencies unless you make it clear to your politician that you want to be included in their advance planning. The politician may be on a list, go to training days and will know which seats are looking for new candidates. They are likely to do a great deal of research and preparation for seats in which they're interested. The spouse or partner is not automatically copied in on that information, especially if the politician is applying to several constituencies at the same time. You can suddenly find your politician in the final stages of the selection process and expecting you to look enthusiastic, when you were barely aware they were applying for that particular seat. Try to avoid this surprise. A lack of enthusiasm on your part, from lack of preparation, or from having heard the same joke once too often, could make a crucial difference to your politician's chances of selection. Unfortunately, first impressions are often the only ones for which there's time on such occasions. Preparation is essential – don't believe anyone who claims to have been selected for a seat without working at it.

Do your homework

If you don't know much about the constituency, explore the background. Read the local paper. Search the Internet. Get to understand the current issues. Find out what the existing MP has been saying. If you talk about the seat with your politician, it will help them consider their responses to questions and will provide you with facts so you can contribute to discussion. Even if it's made clear that no one at a selection meeting is going to ask you questions, it's sensible to be ready with obvious interest in the local area, in case someone breaks ranks. Consider your possible responses well in advance, not at the selection itself. Ask what issues were raised in the earlier rounds of the selection process, too. Find out whether the constituency association has laid down any stipulations which might affect you.

> ❝ I've seen marriages founder because the putative MP agreed to anything and everything in order to get the seat, leaving the spouse to try and fall into line. ❞

Discuss your concerns

It is common to have doubts about whether your politician really ought to be trying to get selected. Not every partner is keen on the idea from the outset. Don't bottle up the concerns you may have. Talk to your politician about them. Weigh up any good or bad aspects of the plans and discuss the choices in advance. You may not have the luxury of much time for discussion after they've been selected, and it will be too late to do much about it by then.

When and whether to attend the selection

Generally, spouses and partners of candidates don't attend the early rounds of the selection process, but when the numbers have been whittled down, you may be invited to go along. Constituencies vary hugely in this respect and many new ideas are being tried with the introduction of special lists and special procedures. The constituency may not be allowed to insist you attend, but remember they might have doubts about the politician who turns up alone, when the others do not. This is supposed to avoid politicians without partners being at a disadvantage, but it's surely unrealistic to think the constituency activists won't be interested to have sight of those spouses and partners who do exist.

> ❝ Selection is the worst part of the whole process – everything else is manageable and fun – most of the time ❞

Sort out the likely logistics

Find out what sort of selection process has been arranged. Don't assume a standard pattern will be followed or that it will be the same as the last one you attended. Just as each constituency is different, so the method of choosing their next candidate will vary. Ask practical questions. Your politician may otherwise not focus on how you fit into the arrangements. What time of day is the meeting taking place? How much time will you have to look around? Will you be staying overnight? (If so, it's a good idea to take a choice of clothes so you look comfortable whatever the weather conditions on the next day, and whatever the activities.) There might be an informal part of the selection process, where you mingle with constituency activists, or you might just be on view on a platform at a general meeting. (Always assume you are going to be seated on a raised platform, with no table in front of your legs, and dress accordingly. There is every chance you'll be photographed from an unflattering angle.) It's possible you may need to be prepared for outdoor activity, such as a canvassing exercise or walkabout.

Personal questions to you

If there's an informal part to the selection procedure, it may allow candidates, with their partners, to meet and talk to some of the constituency activists. Advance thought about likely topics for conversation is a good idea. Some people may ask apparently rude personal questions about your work, political views, or personal plans. It's often difficult to distinguish between hostile and curious questioning. The person asking the question may well be supporting one of the other candidates and may be seeking to rile you. Equally, such questions could just be inelegant conversational gambits. If you give your questioner's motives the benefit of the doubt, you are more likely to avoid difficulties. Try not to take exception to inquisitiveness, even if it seems very personal (then, if they wanted to rile you, you'll have disappointed them). Be absolutely honest in everything you say. Avoid being or sounding evasive. What you tell them is bound to be remembered and may be repeated later, especially if your politician has unwittingly expressed divergent views.

Your politician's views

Be wary of a person asking you what your politician thinks about a particular issue. They will probably be asking because, for them, it's a burning issue and that will probably mean it will be controversial locally. Remember that they really want to know the politician's views,

9

not yours, and may not have been able to ask the politician direct. Even if you think you know the answer, it's usually better to suggest they put it direct. Ask their name and introduce them to the politician, if you have the opportunity.

Public questions affecting you

If you're visibly attending the selection meeting, whether on a platform or at the back of the room, questions may be directed to your politician which involve you and which you may want to answer, even if you've been told you won't be expected to say anything. It will help if you've thought about issues which might arise, so you aren't caught out. The politician who looks across the room in anguish when asked a tricky question about joint plans may not convey a reassuring message to the meeting. Discuss with your politician beforehand whether you might like to reply. For instance, you might like to answer questions about practical arrangements – where you'll live, where your children will go to school, how much you'll be involved – but not on political topics. If you do give answers, be absolutely clear and don't equivocate. If speaking in public is really not for you, make sure your politician knows they will need to answer everything on your behalf.

Meeting the other spouses and partners

One of the daunting features of each selection process can be meeting the other candidates and their spouses or partners. They may make you feel thoroughly inferior, giving the impression of knowing exactly what they're doing and being a certainty to win that candidacy. Gamesmanship is rife in these situations. Some may be former MPs and will appear to be enormously more experienced than your politician. Try to suppress the natural instinct to treat the others as hostile rivals. The chances are some of the other politicians will end up as candidates and MPs in other seats, and those spouses and partners will then be your future colleagues. Being friendly at each selection will be remembered and can reap dividends. It also provides good practice for coping with the successes and failures of later political life.

First impressions: only impressions

The selection meeting is not supposed to be a beauty contest, but you could be forgiven for feeling your part in it is just that. When you talk to activists later about why they voted for your politician, you might be dismayed at the apparent triviality of the reasons given. "You looked so interested in what was being said." "You laughed at the jokes." "I liked what you were wearing." And so on. Those, of course, may not be their

11

real reasons (and there's every chance they didn't actually vote for your politician) but that may be all those people remember about your involvement. It's a salutary reminder about your peripheral role in the process. They are selecting the politician, not you.

Failure to be selected

If your politician is unsuccessful, you will need to jettison all your cherished plans for that constituency and instantly regroup. Look to the future, instead of reading great significance into the circumstances of the rejection. Restrain any temptation to condemn the tactics of the winner and their supporters, even to close friends, since you will not alter the result and are more likely to saddle your politician with a reputation for being an ungracious loser. It's helpful to have a contingency plan ready as it's hard to be constructive when you're just as cross as they are. You may find you're the only person comforting your politician. They may despair for a while, fearing no constituency will ever select them. That seldom lasts long, and they will soon either be racing off to the selection process for the next possible seat, or discovering a burning ambition to do something completely different. Perhaps even something outside politics: in which case, read no further.

Successful selection: the loss of autonomy

If your politician is successful, you will probably face immediate and dramatic changes in your life. Straight after the selection meeting, you may find the local association assumes ownership of your politician, whisking them away to a round of press interviews, visits and events. It's possible you will feel a bit excluded. You are no longer the sole cheer leader. You've become the bag carrier, bringing up the rear and left to sort out the mundane domestic arrangements. Don't be dismayed: this is quite normal. It's vital for the new candidate to get as much publicity as quickly as possible. Be prepared for this sudden change and don't take personal affront.

Suspend your own ego?

One male spouse observed that the crucial point for a man in the spouse's role was to suspend his ego whenever required. In fact, that's good advice to all spouses and partners through most of the political process. You are there to support, not to share the limelight, in the constituency. The temptation to leap in with your own advice or to answer a question (particularly in an area where you have special knowledge) ought to be resisted, even in informal conversation. It can be embarrassing to see your personal private views being reported, often inaccurately, in a newspaper, as if they were the views of your politician. But that is not to say you need to be invisible and remain silent right from the start when the candidate is selected. There is bound to be some curiosity about the spouse or partner of the new candidate. A few interesting and relevant paragraphs about your personal history in a press release may help clarify your politician's image. Discuss with your politician and the agent what might be said and keep editorial control if at all possible.

> ❝ It's a difficult balance to strike between being entertaining and saying nothing interesting. I am still learning.❞

The incumbent spouse or partner

After selection, if your politician hopes to succeed an incumbent, you may be encouraged to speak to the spouse or partner of the current MP. Remember that they may have mixed feelings about the transition: upset about losing status; relief at stepping out of the glare; concern about how you will perform; and so forth. Much of their local knowledge will be invaluable, though, so it's well worth talking. Work out what questions you have for them, rather than simply listening to what they say. Assess their advice in the light of your own plans. If there is expected to be a long period until the election, you will need to collaborate about your respective roles so that you complement one another.

Consulting all predecessors in a testing ground

If the seat where your politician has been selected is safe for another party, with a huge majority to overturn, it's possible that no politician will be standing at more than one election there. It can be very instructive to seek out the partners of the previous few candidates for a chat, especially if they played a significant part in the earlier campaigns. Such insights will be really helpful to you both. How your politician tackles the challenges of that seat can have a real impact on their prospects of being selected in another, more winnable, seat after the election, if they are unsuccessful this time round.

Shouldering domestic arrangements

After being selected for a seat, lots of new domestic arrangements do have to be made. The organisation of many or all will fall on your shoulders. It is useful to have discussed them in outline with your politician before their focus shifts onto campaigning.

At home

Living in the constituency?

The issue of where a parliamentary politician's family makes its home raises blood pressure higher than almost any other issue of concern to spouses and partners, and needs to be considered openly right from the start. Some constituencies make a 'local home' a stipulation for being selected. There are many reasons why a home in the constituency is useful prior to being elected, but, equally, it may not be possible or necessary for everyone.

> ❝ If my husband is going to be an MP for the next twenty years or so, then I want it to work in the best possible way for my family – it's sure as hell an awful long time to sulk! ❞

The need to canvass and campaign

Canvassing and campaigning can be time consuming, particularly in the evenings and at weekends, when potential electors are most likely to be at home. The commitment of the candidate to such activity is vital and it can be difficult to achieve without a home base in the constituency. A guaranteed programme of personal presence on specific evenings or specific weekends might be a satisfactory alternative. Find out how much campaigning the constituency association organises on a regular basis.

Involvement in local life

Empathy with local electors is another reason often given for the candidate needing to live in the constituency. Many politicians agree that living in the constituency gives them a special feel for local issues as they arise. If the family is not physically there, the electors need some strong reassurance that the candidate truly understands their local concerns. This can be especially important if one of the other parties has chosen a local councillor to fight the seat, since they can agitate about key issues from a position of authority and local experience. They'll also use every opportunity to attack your politician for not being 'local'.

Involvement in local politics

You or your politician might consider standing for the local council and that has a specific legal requirement for a local home address.

Past experience and changing lifestyles

Bear in mind, though, that there may be an element of inertia involved in a stipulation about living in the constituency. Activists may expect their politician to make their main home in the constituency simply because that is what their previous MP did, without taking into account the many changes in family structure which have taken place over the decades since they last selected a candidate. It was more common in the past for families to have a single bread winner and for spouses and children to move wherever the earner's work took them, with the children changing schools at any stage of the academic cycle. For some diplomats and foreign correspondents that can still be the case. Some older activists have a mental image of their perfect candidate along those lines, but if you talk to them about the lifestyles of their own adult children, you may discover they accept that times have changed for a different generation. Other arrangements can be just as efficient for nursing and winning a seat.

Home address on the ballot paper

Having a local home address on the General Election ballot paper is another factor in favour of a home in the constituency. There is some anecdotal evidence that a non-local address will deter some electors when their pencil hovers over the ballot paper in the voting booth, particularly if other local or regional elections are happening at the same time and they have more than one vote to cast. It will certainly be commented upon.

What is a 'home address'?

As a matter of electoral law, it's a strict requirement that the nomination paper and the ballot paper give the candidate's 'home' address. But, what constitutes 'home' for this purpose? There are no hard and fast definitions, but it does have to be a proper home. A candidate cannot simply rent a spare room in a local house for the duration of the campaign and put that down as their home address. A candidate needs to make sure the home address they give, whether rented or owned, is where they regularly sleep, cook meals, and have their possessions. It will also probably be where their family lives for some or all of the time. It is not a legal requirement, though, for the candidate and family to live solely in the constituency. Electoral law makes it clear a candidate can possess more than one 'home' address at any one time, provided that each of those home addresses is genuinely used as a home during that period by the candidate. This will be the case for many sitting MPs, who have homes both at Westminster and in the constituency. (Times have rather changed from the older election law which provided '*ubi uxor ibi domus*' – 'home is where the wife is'. That meant a candidate did not actually need to be living at a constituency address at all to call it his 'home', provided his wife lived there. That no longer applies.)

> ❝ It was a long time ago and we're still together ... I had to move, single handed and heavily pregnant, to a part of the world where it seemed to snow for six months of the year. ❞

Family finances and family views

For some candidates with financial constraints, the consideration about whether either of two homes might be regarded as 'home', in election law, can be pretty academic. The choices while fighting a seat may be between continuing to live in the constituency, moving to the constituency or continuing to live elsewhere and visiting. For every family, different preferences and constraints apply. Talk them through well in advance of making promises to a constituency. In particular, bring older children into the discussion. They are likely to have strong views, especially about their schooling, and a failure to consult may blight family life.

Contesting the seat is at your expense

There are a number of misconceptions you may encounter which have a bearing on housing arrangements. One is that party finance is available to enable candidates to pay for second homes while they are nursing seats, along the lines of trades union sponsorship. Another is that only wealthy people, able to afford two homes, put themselves forward as candidates. The facts are usually very different. For some candidates, financial constraints may be so great that they cannot afford to buy or rent somewhere in the constituency when they are first selected. Financial difficulties will probably be understood by an association, but extra reassurance about planned devotion to the constituency and campaigning will be essential.

A place of your own

If you do not live in the constituency, people may initially offer to put you and your politician up overnight, so you can attend evening events. It is wise not to overstay your welcome or presume on their hospitality too frequently. You really do need to find somewhere to stay as your own base, where you can talk freely to one another and not be on 'best behaviour'.

Risks of the housing market

If you decide to move your sole home to the constituency, once selected, remember you will be at the mercy of the electorate and the prevailing political climate. The politician might not be elected at the next election. If you have sold your home in a more expensive area and moved to the constituency, you may find it very difficult to return to the original area if prices have risen disproportionately in the meantime. Nursing a marginal seat can therefore prove very costly. But your politician may have concluded it is only by buying a property and living there that they can demonstrate they truly expect to win the seat.

Single focus before election: dual focus afterwards

In family terms, the pre-election period is certainly more straight forward if the candidate and family live in the constituency – all under the same roof. But after the election, difficulties may arise if the elected politician spends long hours from Monday to Thursday or Friday at Westminster, and cannot get home each night to the family. If the MP also travels widely, making speeches around the country or attending conferences, the constituency based family may seldom see them, even at weekends. This sort of geographical separation has been blamed for the breakdown of very many parliamentary marriages and relationships. Even if things do not get that bad, there is considerable scope for the spouse or partner left in the constituency to feel lonely and isolated, 'like a single parent', excluded from the 'Westminster Village'. If your choice is to have the main or sole home in the constituency, then you need to talk about these issues in advance and develop strategies for coping.

> ❝ My predecessor but one told me she'd felt like a single parent, bringing up the children on her own in the constituency.
> I decided I was determined not to face that. ❞

Weeks in London: weekends in the constituency

Some political families, particularly those based in London before selection, deal with the change of balance between before and after election, by keeping their London base and also having a home in the constituency. It can be sensible to rent in the constituency at the outset, if that can be afforded, since it might look presumptuous to buy a home before being endorsed by the electorate. That arrangement enables the partner to continue with their existing work and for any children to continue in their existing schools during the week. At weekends and holidays, the whole family can be involved in campaigning in the constituency. After being successfully elected, the politician and family might be able to buy a home in the constituency, and the family could continue to live together near Parliament during the week. The splitting of time between two homes requires careful planning and the purchase of many duplicate household items, but many feel it's much better for family life if the family is together most of the time. True, you are not available mid-week to go to coffee mornings (but if you are working you would not be doing that anyway). The key to making such an arrangement work, and to avoid it being suggested that you are only interested in metropolitan life, is to make sure a good level of constituency activity is highly visible from both you and the politician when you are there. Let the constituency know in advance that that is how you would like to organise your lives.

Don't suffer in silence on your own

One difficulty of making the family's home base in the constituency is that some partners can feel isolated when the politician is at Westminster, but may be worried about discussing how they feel in case it damages the politician's reputation. Local friends so easily spread gossip. Such comments as: "Don't rock the boat!" – "Pretend everything is fine!" are often made, but that just lets problems fester. It's far better to talk to your politician about how you feel, so you can both do something about it. If you can't discuss things, then the failure of communication can be made worse by the geographic separation, and can lead to each of you leading effectively separate lives with limited shared interests and different sets of friends.

Being in touch with other spouses and partners

A central address list with phone numbers and e-mails for spouses and partners does not exist, at present. There is a near impossibility of keeping such details private from junk e-mails and other unwanted intrusion. Although many partners already swap such details informally, that does not always bring new people into the loop, and some can inadvertently be left out, particularly when their politician is newly selected and not yet elected. It is worth persevering with getting in touch with other spouses and partners. You may not get on well with every single one of them, but you are likely to make some real friends, who will really understand the complexities of your life because they have so much in common with you.

> ❝ Maybe offering children interested in contacting other politicians' children a means of doing so would be helpful, so they could compare experiences. ❞

Visiting Westminster

For the spouse or partner based exclusively in the constituency, and not tied to working hours, regular mid-week visits to London might be helpful. MPs do, though, have considerable parliamentary demands during the week and you will need to plan your own entertainment. Get in touch with other spouses or partners in a similar position. 'The Other Half' (formerly 'Conservative Parliamentary Wives') organises trips and meals out. 'Conservative Contact' has speaker meetings. The Commons' facilities are available. There are many other extra-Parliamentary clubs, choirs and other cross-party organisations. Get to know as many people in the political world as possible, both at local and national levels: otherwise you may find the politician coming home and talking about people and events that mean nothing to you.

Transport

Having your own car will mean you are not tied to your politician's travel arrangements, unless the constituency is well served by public transport. Buy two A to Z maps of the constituency, and keep one in the car and one at home. If you travel by train after your politician is elected, there is a scheme which allows you a limited number of train tickets between the constituency and Westminster each year, as part of the MP's expenses.

The home phone number for constituents

Many MPs wish to be easily accessible to their constituents on the telephone. You need to decide how you're going to organise this. If you put your home number in the telephone directory you have to trust that people will respect your openness and only phone at odd hours in an absolute emergency. That is the experience of many, indeed it has the advantage of encouraging children to answer the phone politely from an early age. On the other hand, there is a risk your non-political time may be endlessly invaded and personal calls may be missed. It's a good idea to have a private telephone number for family use. Don't assume it will stay wholly private, though, since it will probably appear on school address lists, and be given out to constituents. If you are in the constituency during the week, and the politician is in Westminster, you may find you have to act as a messaging

service, which is not exactly 'instant access' for the constituents. If you are employed as the politician's secretary or personal assistant, of course, you may be happy to receive constituents' calls at home. If you are going to be on your own, organise a facility giving you the incoming number and allowing you to record calls. It can be a good idea to encourage the politician to give a 'work' mobile number to any journalists who need to contact them. If radio interviews are going to be given by telephone, they will almost certainly need a land line.

An office phone number

If the politician wants to have a direct local line on which constituents can contact them day or night, it is wise to get a specific separate number, equipped with an answering machine or an automatic divert to the politician's office or mobile phone, so you are not constantly being asked to take messages when they are not there. After election, the politician could provide constituents with the direct number of their Westminster office, which has an out of hours answering and paging service. Another possibility is to have a telephone number at the constituency office, with an answer machine, which could either be answered by someone manning the office, or accessed remotely by the politician.

The choice of schools for children

Another area of considerable controversy surrounds the education of politicians' children. Some politicians like saying their children are educated in local constituency schools, demonstrating empathy with the electorate. Others believe it important to use state education rather than private education. Those are, essentially, adult and financial choices. The real question is: what is the best choice for the child? Will they thank you if decisions are taken about their education which have more of an eye on political advantage than their best interests? Don't panic about getting it right from the outset, though. If you find you've made the wrong choice initially, the move from junior to senior school is often a good time to reconsider locations, as between the constituency and London.

School in the constituency

At a local school, children are sometimes singled out as being the children of the 'local MP' and may find bullying, taunting or nagging quite a problem. Children need to know this often happens, so they don't take it personally. It can be very hard, too, for children to give neutral responses to probing questions about family life. They, and you, can often regret too much frankness. The fact they are in constituency schools will also probably mean they do not see the politician parent much while Parliament is sitting, except possibly at weekends.

School near Westminster

When a politician's family lives with them near Westminster during the week, the children can have relative anonymity in London schools. They may see a little more of the politician parent during the week, although 'family friendly hours' tend not to include children's teatime. The downside of London schools is that school friends and social activities will usually be London based and this can cause conflict when your family weekends are spent in the constituency, especially for older children. Inviting friends to stay at weekends is one solution. Providing interesting activities in the constituency is another.

The boarding school option

For some political families, boarding school is the right answer. The children can effectively escape from political life completely during term time. This can also give you greater freedom to be with the politician both at Westminster and in the constituency.

Attending children's school events

Currently, while Parliament is sitting, it is safest to assume your politician will need to be at Westminster from mid-day till evening Monday to Thursday, when votes may take place. (The hours are different each day, and keep changing, so you'll need to check precise hours regularly.) Mornings are likely to be taken up with committees, meetings and constituency business. Many MPs will attend dinners in the early evening and they may be making speeches. Even if children are in London during the week, they and you may see relatively little of the politician. Although MPs can sometimes obtain dispensation from the

Whips to attend children's parents' evenings, plays or sports days, you cannot guarantee this will always happen. It is usually easier for the politician to attend such events if they are in London, because they do not need to take so long away from the office and can then return to parliamentary business.

Assumptions about children's political views

At senior levels in schools and at University, older children may find that teachers or lecturers attempt to engage them in political discussion as if the young person's views exactly mirror those of their political parent. Children need to be warned about this in advance, so they do not feel misunderstood or picked upon. If, on the other hand, they have their own very different political views, they should be encouraged to emphasise that those are their own views and not those of the political parent.

Babysitting arrangements

Attending evening political events is made much easier if you have regular and reliable babysitting arrangements in place. If you are new to a constituency and have no local family who can help, it's a good idea to ask the constituency chairman or the agent if they can recommend a reliable person. Find out the local going rate and always offer to pay it. Some people may be reluctant to ask for payment, but that does not mean you should presume on their generosity. In addition, having babysitting arrangements which give you the option to spend some child-free time with your politician can be good for you both.

Religion: a rotation system

Some politicians operate a rotation system of visiting every major place of worship in their constituency in turn. This has advantages in terms of visibility, but can have disadvantages if more devout worshippers conclude that the politician is insincere. It can also confuse your children about their religious identity if you show no consistency to them.

Religion: the single place of worship

Other politicians develop a strong connection with a single place of worship in the constituency. While they will not be being particularly visibly religious anywhere else, they may find their own religious views better served and their children may develop a better sense of a religious identity. By the nature of political commitments, though, it may not be possible to visit each and every week, so there's still a risk that the more devout worshippers there will conclude the politician does not share their level of devotion.

Shopping with the politician

If the politician is with you, shopping in a constituency supermarket or the local shops always seems to take longer than you planned. Constituents will approach saying "I know this isn't a good moment, but I just wanted to ask….". You won't want to appear rude, so make sure you know whether your politician would like you to stay with them (with the risk one of your children may complain embarrassingly or ask who the person is, when you don't know). The alternative is to move on with the shopping trolley and the children, and let the politician catch up when they can.

Shopping anonymously?

In some places, constituents seem insatiably fascinated by what you have in your shopping trolley. This is a curious feature of being a minor local celebrity: try not to let it irritate you. Even if you think you have kept yourself nicely anonymous in a big supermarket, you will often find people saying later that they saw you there. Remember this when the children are playing up, or you have been treated badly by a shop assistant and feel like making a fuss.

Going to non-political local activities and events

If you get to know as much of the constituency as possible, you will develop a better understanding of what the politician is trying to achieve for the local people. The more effort you put in to visiting local clubs and organisations and to taking part in annual activities, not just political events, the more information you will have about the mood and views of the constituents. Listen and be sympathetic and keep notes of important details. Don't assume your politician knows all about every local issue. You may well be given a piece of important information at such an event which they don't know. Try, though, to keep such bits of news succinct when you pass them on.

> 66 People assume you're the font of all knowledge and ring you up to recommend the best local florist. 99

The Constituency organisation and activities

The people: who does what

At an early stage, it's a good idea to work out how the particular constituency organisation operates. This varies hugely from place to place and changes with time. There may be a paid agent, part or full-time, perhaps shared with another constituency. There may be other part time staff or volunteers. There will almost always be a constituency chairman and other constituency officers, all volunteers, who tend to be in office for 3 years at a time. There may be chairmen and officers of some or all of the individual branches (the subdivisions, in the constituency). You need to find out how many active branches there are, and keep in mind that this will change from time to time. Try to get a feel for the relative strengths of the individuals. If you talk to as many of them as possible and keep their relevant phone numbers and e-mail addresses to hand, you will always be prepared. Most constituencies produce a list of names, addresses and phone numbers of officers, branch chairmen, activists etc. Get your own copy. It can prove invaluable, especially for compiling Christmas card lists. Keep in mind, though, that the first names recorded on such lists are not always the names or diminutives by which those people prefer to be known.

> ❝ I met one candidate's wife who kept a card index with names, vital statistics and recent operations in it. 'Fred Smith, married to Joan, recently had a hip operation' - must be fantastic if it works and you don't put the wrong face to the wrong name and botch the type of operation completely! ❞

Name recognition

Do your best to learn the names of those you encounter in the local association and constituency, but don't be afraid to admit you can't remember everyone. It sometimes helps to remember a salient fact about each person: their job, their recent operation, their sporting interest. Similarly, don't make the assumption that everyone automatically knows who you are. If you have a different surname, it's a good idea not to confuse people by using it to introduce yourself, without adding the tag of your relationship to the politician.

Helping keep activists happy

Always bear in mind that constituency activists are volunteers and are crucial to the election or re-election of your politician. Say thank you when someone has helped you and write letters after special events (unless you and the politician have agreed that the 'thank you' is more appreciated if it comes direct from the politician). We all know activists who have drifted away from the association in pique because they felt under-valued. If you encourage people to speak out, if you or the politician has upset someone, then it's easier to put things right. Try not to take sides in internal arguments between activists.

> **❝** One of the best things a spouse can do is to be an additional pair of eyes and ears - spot who is out of sorts and may need a word of encouragement or thanks or notice which two committee members have fallen out with each other, and warn the politician. **❞**

Messages for the politician

Unless you really intend to be a direct and reliable conduit for all messages to the politician, it's a good idea to discourage people from telling you something which they expect you to pass on to the politician. Plead a dreadful memory and urge them to speak or e-mail direct to the politician, if it's important. You cannot know which pieces of information are vital and which can safely be filtered out; and you risk irritating your politician if you continually pass on dull moans or, worse, if you unintentionally fail to mention something of the utmost importance.

Conversational traps to avoid

It's easy to say you need to develop a thick skin if you are involved in politics, but it's hard to achieve. Try not to be upset by unintended slights and thoughtless comments. You may have your own professional expertise in some specific field and find yourself being treated to less than well-formed views on a subject about which you know far more. Some people find it a challenge if you put them right. (Others, though, may realise you have interesting views and will enjoy a serious discussion with you.) It can be extremely difficult to tread the line between being controversial and being entertaining. When meeting someone for the first time, err on the side of caution. In addition, be wary of moaning about your life as a spouse or partner, even in fun. Throwaway comments have been known to start false rumours of imminent divorce.

Becoming involved in local constituency politics

You may feel you'd like to become involved in council politics in the constituency. Even if you don't plan to become involved, you might be encouraged to put your name forward as a 'paper' candidate. Don't do either, unless you're keen to get into local politics – you might get elected unexpectedly, and you need to be sure you can commit yourself to the hours of council attendance and the surgeries required. Keep in mind that an MP with a councillor spouse or partner in the same constituency can experience difficulties if there are local contentious issues on which you have different perspectives.

What if you are also a candidate or MP?

A spouse or partner of a politician can themselves be a candidate or an MP. The best advice from those with experience of this is to maintain a very clear dividing line between your own political responsibility and your provision of support for your other half. This is probably no different to the balancing act required in most relationships, where each provides a supporting role to the other's career, but it gains greater attention if both of you are in the public eye and because there are still relatively few such couples. Precise logistics will depend on how close the constituencies are to one another. It's important that both constituencies know what to expect from their politician, and also that they only look to their own politician for answers to questions, not to the partner. You may find both constituencies are more ready to accept that they'll probably not see the other politician at branch events, than they would if a non-political career were involved.

> ❝ Find out whether you're expected at an event, even if your name isn't on the invitation. The politician may be given the bunch of flowers intended for you. ❞

Identifying the range of constituency events

As a spouse or partner, you're likely to find yourself expected to attend all manner of fund raising events and parties. Depending on the zeal of your constituency and its various branches, there may be speaker meetings; dinners; drinks parties; safari suppers; quiz nights; opera evenings; carol concerts; summer fairs; jumble sales; auctions; coffee mornings and etc. etc. There are no hard and fast rules about whether you and the politician should pay for your entrance to each such event, but it can become extremely expensive if you pay each time. If you are being obliged to attend as support for your politician, when you would not otherwise attend, you should not really be expected to pay. When first involved in a constituency, you may feel you ought to attend every branch or ward event, to meet as many people as possible. This is bound to raise expectations of future attendance, especially if you go to an annual event two years running. In order to 'start as you mean to go on', try to find out from the agent or constituency chairman roughly what numbers of events you are likely to encounter in the course of a year and work out how many you can realistically attend. Everyone has to find their own balance between diligence and exhaustion.

The local importance of branch events

If each branch has only one main event in the year, its members will assume you look forward to attending as much as they do. They will like you to be there, so they can talk to both the politician and to you, while perhaps not appreciating that there may be dozens of other branch events which you are also 'expected' to attend. Whilst these events generally have a fund raising element, they are also regarded as something pleasurable by the members of the particular branch. It is tactful to keep this in mind. If a branch persistently holds events at a time or on a day of the week when you cannot attend, and they would like you to be there, suggest a time you can manage and then stick to it.

Civic duties

There will also be a range of civic and non-party political events in the constituency to which you may be invited. These frequently follow an annual pattern and the agent, constituency chairman or your predecessor may be able to tell you what you can expect. If the constituency covers more than one local authority area, you may have to rotate attendance at Remembrance services or Mayoral ceremonies because of clashes.

> ❝ I do think it's important to carve out your own ground rules early on, rather than accepting what you think is expected of you. ❞

Setting the expectations for your wider political involvement

Other types of political activity may also interest you. If you like making speeches, giving fund raising dinner parties, chairing meetings or making produce for sales, that's something you should pursue. But you may find the constituency activists expect you to continue to do those things indefinitely, if you do them too frequently. Helping with the washing up at every event is another way of storing up difficult expectations (but is often welcomed, if you have the time and dexterity). If you keep your schedule flexible and make it understood you are not starting a precedent each time you do something, you may avoid raising unreasonable expectations. In particular, choose early on whether to retain your home as a private place or to use it for political entertaining.

> 66 Because I work full time and travel a lot, he told the constituency from the outset to expect me when they saw me. It set the tone. So now, when I'm around, they consider it a bonus and if I'm not, they don't call the 'News of the World'. 99

Being compared unfavourably with your predecessor

If the previous politician's spouse or partner attended every event (or managed to convey that impression) then you may find there's an assumption you'll do the same. If you're not able to, be prepared to explain the differences in approach, kindly, to anyone who's interested, while still making it clear you are wholly supportive. There are bound to be mutterings that you are a disappointment, but you should persevere, and they will hopefully come to terms with your different personality.

The complications of there being no dress code

Before any event, try to obtain the invitation or flier and find out if you are expected to wear anything special. Nothing obliges you to follow instructions, but you may find you want to conform when 'on parade' and avoid embarrassment. These days, there are no general rules about dress. Some people will always wear hats for particular events, while others avoid them. Some people like wearing jeans or

leggings when being informal in the constituency: others do not. Some abide by a constituency discouragement about wearing red: others decide it suits them and make a point of wearing it. If you are consistently unconventional, the theory is that people will grow accustomed with time. Some spouses and partners, though, never quite manage to stop feeling over- or under-dressed at events and you should not regard this as a failure.

Contributing raffle prizes

'Start as you mean to go on' especially applies to things like raffle prizes. Unless you plan to take a raffle prize to every single event you attend, don't start the habit and then tail off. There is, after all, no central repository of free raffle prizes for politicians to dole out. Such things come out of your own financial resources.

Buying at fairs

If there is a constituency fair or sale, with many different stalls run by different branches, you may feel under an obligation to buy something from each stall, to keep people happy. This can be prohibitively expensive and you may acquire many things you don't really need. It is more sensible to head straight for the stalls where you're likely to find things you'd like to have: books, plants, cakes etc. and then to be seen at other stalls already laden down with bags and clearly taking an enthusiastic part in the event in general.

Don't judge competitions

It is widely recommended that you should never agree to judge any sort of competition, irrespective of your own personal expertise and however flattering the invitation. You will only please one person and will disgruntle the rest. You can, of course, hand out prizes, after another judge has courted the opprobrium of making choices.

Raffle etiquette

Do draw the raffle, if you are asked. Sometimes you will find this is the only action expected of you at an event. If a number of different colours of raffle tickets have been used, make sure you chose descriptions for each of the colours that can't be misheard: avoiding, for example, 'green' and 'cream'. To avoid the disapproval of drawing the ticket for the top prize for yourself, you could buy a few tickets, but discreetly not take them, or you could give them to someone else. If there is a table of prizes to choose from, it is uncontroversial to choose a modest prize if your ticket is drawn. Avoid re-cycling the item at the next raffle, lest you

offend the donor. If more than one of your tickets is drawn, it's always polite to decline to take a second prize. If there are a very large number of prizes to be distributed, draw two or three tickets at a time, to prevent the draw going on too long, but keep an eye on each ticket to make sure the prizes are collected, so you don't disappoint the holders of the last few tickets drawn, who may find there are no prizes left.

Children and branch events

If you have small children, you may find it accepted that you and they will only attend a few big events each year. In some political families, the politician tends to attend a branch event with just one of the children, but not the whole family. Some political families decide that apart from Christmas carol concerts and Remembrance Sunday, there is no good reason for their children to attend constituency or public activities, at all. With good child minding arrangements, that can be made to work. In any case, as children get older, their own social arrangements will mean they're less likely to attend unless they decide to for themselves.

Children and publicity

If children attend public events, there is a possibility they will be photographed. Although there are general restrictions on the press use of such photographs, you may wish to discourage publication to preserve their privacy. Some local newspaper editors will understand this request and will abide by it. If that is your wish, let the children know, so they can turn away from a camera without feeling they are being rude.

> ❝ If you want to preserve their privacy, don't parade your family, however proud you are of them. ❞

Feeding children at branch events

Fund raising events rarely involve food which small children will eat, apart from bread and butter. It's a good idea to make special arrangements and let the organisers know if you are bringing children. Offer suggestions if they are especially picky about food. The alternative is to feed them before you set off, so they aren't hungry and will be happy just grazing on puddings. If you take children to an annual event one year, but not the next, make sure you let the organisers know the children are not coming on the second occasion, or you may be greeted with plates of sausages and concerned enquiries about their well-being.

Keep the freezer stocked

Give consideration to your own food, as well. You or the politician may sometimes be so busy at election time or at events, talking to people or keeping an eye on your children, that you do not have much chance to eat or enjoy any of the food. A range of meals in the freezer can swiftly fill gaps when you return home. If you think you will not have much time to eat at an event, having some food beforehand will keep you going and avoid suggestions of greediness which might follow if you wolf plates of canapés.

> ❝ You can spend so long talking and circulating at functions that you'll barely eat. Great if you're on a diet, but not good for your stamina. ❞

Keep the children busy at branch events

The sad truth is that children are rarely gripped by political discourse in the same way as adults. They get tired of being told how much they've grown, or of having to explain they're not doing GCSEs yet because they're only 11. If you want to avoid them getting fractious and asking loudly when they can go home, plan ahead with activities. If there is a safe garden, perhaps they could go out to play in it. (Have a spare set of clothes in the car just in case they fall in a ditch or get very muddy.) A friendly dog might need some exercise. A children's or grandchildren's upstairs room in the house might have videos suitable for them to watch. A computer might be a convenient distraction. Some older children find events easier to cope with if they have a task such as handing round plates of food, or if they can bring a friend of the same age (but check with the friend's parents to make sure they don't object to exposure to politics). It is helpful, too, if the children can be discouraged from interrupting the politician's speech.

Babies at branch events

People like cooing at politicians' beautifully behaved babies, but don't always think about the facilities needed. If you take a baby to a political event, you may want to make sure there is a spare room where the baby can be fed, changed or put down to sleep in peace. Being some distance

away will mean that howls of misery won't disrupt the politician's speech. Remember that not everyone is comfortable with public displays of breast feeding.

Standing in for the politician

Some spouses and partners who are based in the constituency, stand in for the politician at local events which the politician cannot attend because they take place mid-week. This is only feasible if you don't work or can easily take time off. You ought to make it clear from the outset whether you are potentially available for such tasks. If, for example, work means you cannot attend funerals because of the short notice inevitably involved, then that might be a type of occasion you can never manage, even if you can attend other events with a longer notice period. In some constituencies, such substitution is discouraged because it suggests the politician has not been bothered to come themselves. If that's the case, the event will need to be specially arranged to fit in with the politician's other duties.

> ❝ Keep the politician down to earth - make sure the public mask they put on for official life doesn't get stuck on them. ❞

The misconceptions about free time

It is a common public misconception that parliamentary politicians only work from Monday to Thursday and have the rest of the time free. In fact, many work all day Friday, Saturday and Sunday, as well, in the constituency or nationally, in one role or another, and frequently have no organised free time. Even if you do not attend all events with the politician, you and your family will be affected by this lifestyle.

Keeping each Sunday or one weekend a month free

Trying to carve out some personal or family time from a politician's schedule requires delicate negotiation. Some political families operate a diary that keeps every Sunday free. This can be difficult to establish after a period of intensive nursing of the seat, where campaigning may only have been possible at weekends, but it can be pointed out, once the politician has been elected, that they will be working at Westminster from Monday to Thursday or Friday and will need to have at least one day a week with their families. Those who have achieved this speak very positively of its benefits for family life, and say their constituencies understand that if they want the politician at a branch event, they should not hold it on a Sunday. Of course there are exceptions – Remembrance Day services, Mayoral Sundays and so on. Another method of time management is to keep one whole weekend free each month, and to be rigorous in preserving it for family and non-political activities.

Weekends in January and August

There can be a flurry of local events before Christmas and in June or July which may leave you feeling shattered. Weekends in January and August might then be easier to keep free, so you can recover together.

Have at least one proper holiday

It is worth making sure you have one good holiday each year. Uninformed criticism about the length of Parliamentary recesses provokes hollow laughter amongst spouses and partners, who are all too well aware that most MPs work for most of the 'holidays'. Some MPs continue to work even when they're notionally on holiday. Politics can be all consuming and constituents do not stop needing their problems solved, just because Parliament is not sitting. Explaining this over and over again, even if you feel like a school teacher saying that school holidays are taken up with lesson preparation, may eventually get the message across.

The Party Conference and other conferences

Some spouses and partners enjoy accompanying their politician to Party Conference each year. Others would never dream of attending. The choice is yours. Shorter conferences, at weekends, may be easier to manage, if you have work or family commitments. The conferences are useful places to catch up with your fellow spouses and partners because you can swap news in a very condensed space of time. If you want to attend the main conference, even for just one or two days, make early plans because forms need to be filled and countersigned many months in advance, usually through the constituency, to obtain a conference pass. If you are content with attending events outside the security ring, then you won't need a pass and can decide nearer the date. Most parties and meetings, though, are held inside. Some people take very small babies with them to Party Conference, but few seem to repeat the experiment in later years. Comfortable shoes and a light weight rain coat are essentials for most conferences.

The Election

Traditional canvassing and campaigning (for complete beginners):
Spouses and partners are frequently assumed to know every nuance of canvassing and campaigning. It can be embarrassing to confess ignorance, but often if you don't ask you'll never learn. This section may help you with the basics, but every constituency goes about things differently and with the advent of new technologies, methods are constantly being refined.

Your realistic contribution
Attitudes to the involvement of a spouse or partner vary hugely between constituencies. In some places, where there are few activists and those that exist are tied up with their own council elections, unless the spouse or partner takes an active part, little parliamentary campaigning occurs. In other places, there is greater leeway about your involvement. Much will depend on your other commitments to work and family, as well as your own inclination, health and stamina. Discuss it with your politi-

cian, the constituency chairman and the agent. You need to remember, though, that a failure to take any part in the process (unless you have a really good excuse such as imminently giving birth) will raise eyebrows. As with so many aspects of the supportive role, if you start modestly, you can add to that activity later.

> ❝ The key is to under-promise and over-deliver. ❞

Knocking on doors

Canvassing, by knocking on doors and talking to electors, is the traditional means of establishing up to date levels of support for your politician. It can also inform the politician what problems and issues are at the front of electors' minds. You can develop a much closer understanding of the local mood if you hear problems at first hand. The principal purpose, though, is to identify those electors who are definitely going to vote for the candidate, so you can then put your efforts into encouraging just those people and not others to vote on election day. Knocking on doors can be a stressful prospect if you are a shy person. Eulogising your politician's virtues to strangers doesn't come naturally to everyone. Remember you don't have to go canvassing if you really don't want to: there are plenty of other ways you can help. But, equally, don't rule it out without having a go: many partners discover they have a previously unexpected talent. Go out a few times with politicians or an experienced activist and they will show you how it's done.

Identify your party but not yourself

When canvassing in person or by phone, you start by saying which party you're from. It's a good idea not to introduce yourself straight away as the politician's spouse or partner: an elector might be too polite to say they intend voting for another party, and then the wrong information would get recorded and time might be wasted on election day in reminding people to vote who were never planning to vote for your party. There is a risk, as well, that people may be more inclined to berate you, or keep you listening on the doorstep, if they think you'll take their message, whether positive or negative, straight back to the politician.

Canvass cards, rosettes and other equipment

If you canvass in person, wear a rosette to identify your party allegiance and carry the relevant canvass card, with details of each elector taken

from the electoral roll. You need the canvass card because there's no electoral point in calling at houses where there are no registered electors. If you only speak to one person at a house, do not assume all the others in the house necessarily vote the same way. Similarly, if previous voting intention is marked on the card, do not assume they will all vote the same way again, unless they are marked as a current party member. Take the trouble to canvass party members, because they like to be consulted, even if their vote is 'safe'. They often have useful comments on policies. When recording details on the canvass card, it's important to use the correct letters, so the details can be accurately transferred to a master record on paper or computer. A Neighbourhood Watch sign on a door may indicate the household does not welcome personal callers and this may preclude political canvassing, too. Mark the canvass card accordingly, if you decide not to call at that house for that reason.

Telephone canvassing

Another way of canvassing is by telephoning electors. Many spouses and partners find this easier to fit in with other responsibilities, although it is sometimes less satisfactory because it is not so easy to gauge whether someone is giving you truthful information from just the tone of their voice. Body language and eye contact are better indicators. Remember that if the letters TPS (Telephone Preference Service) appear by a name, then that person has asked not to be telephoned in this way. That wish should be respected, even if you also happen to have a telephone number written on the canvass card, since official complaints of breach might embarrass the party.

Predicting the result from canvassing

Individual voting intentions can change over the years and – sometimes – over the course of a campaign, so the canvassing exercise is never perfect. A good canvass, though, can give a reasonable prediction of the likely result and can be used to target particular areas where people are wavering. By comparing it with previous campaign canvasses, it is possible to spot trends in voting intentions. It's therefore a very important tool in the electoral process.

Canvassing an unrepresentative area can depress you

Some parts of a constituency will be better served by activists than others, and those branches with many activists will usually not need help with canvassing. You may well find yourself canvassing an area where there's less expectation of support, and you may become unnecessarily depressed about your politician's chances on the basis of the unrepresentative canvass returns you obtain in those areas. It helps to check in advance the type of area you're being sent to, so you know what to expect. The canvass card may show the previous canvass results, which will give you a good idea.

New systems of voter preference identification

Other more sophisticated systems for identifying possible voting intentions are sometimes used. If these are unfamiliar to activists, a meeting may well be organised at which the system is explained. Make sure you express an interest in attending, so that you can understand what the new system can achieve.

Computer literacy in the constituency office

You might make yourself especially welcome if you become good at troubleshooting computers and programmes in use in the constituency office. Some programmes and pieces of equipment may be relatively elderly if they are only used at election time and have not been replaced due to cost considerations. Not everyone will remember how they were set up at the last election. If you take notes from someone who knows, that information can be invaluable next time. This is especially important if there is a complicated procedure for such things as printing NCRs at the last minute, the night before the election, when computer engineers are not readily available.

Helping prepare leaflets

Apart from canvassing in person or by phone, there are many other activities where you could make a useful contribution during the election period. Some can be very simple. You will be welcomed if you always join in with leaflet folding or addressing when you find yourself in the constituency office (although in some places this activity is being increasingly mechanised). Making cups of tea or coffee for those doing such activities is also usually welcomed.

Check the spelling

You may not get involved in the composition of any of the election literature, but if you do, be sensitive to the content, grammar, layout and spelling. However well expressed your politician's sentiments may be, they will not carry authority if they are incorrectly spelled or messily laid out. Checking those small points can sometimes be a hugely valuable task, and may well be missed by others, if literature is being produced swiftly and they are concentrating on the content.

What to put on election leaflets: family photos

There is a considerable division between those who firmly believe a politician's family picture should appear on every election address and those who insist there is nothing more ghastly than terrible toothy group photos. If you allow pictures of your children to be posted on a web-site, or to appear in election literature, you should be aware that the pictures may be copied or misused. Pictures of children also date very quickly, causing much embarrassment.

A stock of photographs of the politician

If you are good at taking photographs, it can often be helpful to have a running selection of pictures of the politician taken at different events (preferably on a digital camera) which can be used on election litera-ture. Relying on photographs taken by local newspaper photographers may be risky, since they cannot be used without permission, and that is not always forthcoming quickly enough when an election is called.

Investigate other politicians' leaflets

If in doubt about what sorts of photographs and poses work for election literature, browse the Internet for the different sites of individual candi-dates, and look to see how they've presented themselves. Some of their photos would make you want to vote: others will make you wince. It's also useful to keep a folder of old election literature, good and bad, from every election in which you are involved.

Delivering leaflets

Once the leaflets are printed, they'll need to be distributed. There is usually one 'free post' delivery to be prepared for each General Election. Other leaflets will need to be delivered by hand, since the cost of individual postage will be too high for election expenses. Delivering leaflets can be a useful way of getting to know parts of the constituency you may not have previously visited. It also gives you exercise. If it happens to be an area that hasn't been canvassed, then you can usefully note any political posters in windows, and report the information back, without doing a formal canvass.

Letter boxes, dogs, gates and other problems

You need two free hands to deliver leaflets if you're to avoid gashing your fingers or scrunching up the literature. Letter boxes come in many designs and at different heights, but most require one hand to hold the flap (or flaps) open and the other hand to push the leaflet through, particularly if the leaflet is flimsy. Some of the spring mechanisms on letter boxes are vicious and can snap on unwary fingers. Gloves protect the hands but make it difficult to separate the leaflets if worn on both. Be particularly careful to make sure any plasters on your fingers, from previous letter box injuries, are really secure before you deliver further leaflets. Make a note of any house where you can't deliver a leaflet because of a dog who looks dangerous – it may be possible for someone to deliver the leaflet when the dog is not loose.

Gate mechanisms are often idiosyncratic and can sometimes snap shut unexpectedly. Always try to deliver to each flat or room of a communal building, rather than leaving a bundle of leaflets in an entrance hall with a warden or porter.

Delivering in the rain

Have a large waterproof satchel or bag to carry the leaflets, rather than holding them in your hands. If it looks like rain, wear a hooded jacket or waterproof hat, as you will probably not be able to manage an umbrella. Sometimes you will be delivering named and addressed leaflets and it is a good idea to get them into proper delivery order before you set out so you can identify the next address while standing in the previous porch, and not have to walk the same length of pavement twice to deliver one you've missed.

> ❝ It helped enormously when I had a child in a pushchair when out delivering as I could carry leaflets on the buggy. ❞

Election Music

Travelling around in a car during an election period can involve the candidate listening to too much news coverage. It's sometimes good for them to be distracted. You could record a tape or CD, or programme an iPod, to play their favourite range of music, perhaps with a theme relating to the election.

Political balloons and children

Sometimes there may be an opportunity to hand out political balloons. Children often enjoy doing this, provided they know they have their own special balloon waiting for them to take home: otherwise you can experience a reluctance to give the last one out and tears might spoil the occasion.

Organising election help from relatives and friends

Relatives and friends may want to help during the election, but may not know what is expected of them, especially if this is the first election your politician has fought. It's not always easy for the politician to keep a note of all their offers and fit them into the existing organisation, so you may want to co-ordinate that yourself. The able bodied can be encouraged to visit for a day of canvassing, but the more fragile need different tasks. A good cook could be encouraged to prepare a range of easily re-heated meals for the freezer. (You may find you have no time to shop or cook during the election period and the politician may otherwise get unhealthy on a diet of junk food and sweets.) Giving lifts on election day is another possibility. Relatives and friends do need to feel sure they are being useful, otherwise they may not volunteer next time, and these are the people on whom you will want to rely, election after election

Election day committee rooms and NCRs

There are all sorts of sophistications to canvassing, but the basic intention is to identify your supporters in advance of election day. Information from the canvassing returns is collated centrally (manually or on computer) and is then used to generate lists of presumed supporters. These are often typed up with the electoral roll numbers on NCR forms (No Carbon Required) which have several layers of different coloured paper, each bearing the same list of names. These are stuck down on tables in each 'committee room' in electoral roll order. People with postal votes (marked 'av' or 'absent voter') will need to be crossed off the lists. Each committee room may serve one or more polling stations, depending on the manpower available, and a different table is needed for the NCRs for each polling station or polling area.

Traditional Election Day telling and knocking up

There are many different roles you could play on election day. Provided there are sufficient volunteers on the day, 'tellers' wearing plain rosettes without candidates' stickers, situate themselves near the door of each polling station and ask each elector to tell them their electoral roll number (or their address, if they aren't carrying their polling card). Tellers generally 'tell' for an hour or two. The numbers are recorded on pads of 'telling slips' containing space for 20 numbers. Tellers need to be encouraged to make a mark for each elector, whether or not they give their number, so that overall turnout can be monitored as the day progresses. Each hour or so the slips are taken to the committee room, or the numbers can be sent by text, and these are matched against the electoral roll numbers on the NCRs, and a running total of votes for and against is kept. Where a number matches one on the NCR, a line is drawn through that name and number. That line automatically appears on each of the layers below, if you press firmly enough. Later in the day, supporters who do not appear to have voted (because their names have not been crossed off) may be 'knocked up' either with a leaflet through the door or by someone calling at the house to urge them to vote. Because there are several layers to the NCR, if there is sufficient manpower, waves of knocking up can take place during the afternoon and evening right up until the polls close at 10.00 pm. In a tight contest, that can be vital.

Other ways of getting out the vote

That traditional activity is not possible in all constituencies, particularly if there has not been a widespread canvass or there are insufficient volunteers to run committee rooms. A variety of other methods of 'Getting Out The Vote' for your politician may be used. Find out in advance what is planned, so that you can be effective in helping. Offer your services in good time so you can be included in the grid.

Touring the committee rooms

In some constituencies, it's traditional for the politician to spend Election Day visiting each of the committee rooms in turn. This keeps the politician out of the constituency office for the day, and reduces the risk they may fret and irritate those co-ordinating the campaign. You might well accompany them, if you're not needed in a committee room. If you do this, it would be useful to make a list, in the order of planned visit, of the addresses of the committee rooms, with up to date contact phone numbers and contact names. There are two schools of thought about letting each committee room know when you plan to visit. If you tell each group the time, then there's a risk no one will be out knocking up at that time, and if you run late the problem of people lingering is compounded. You may, though, find this actually makes you run even later, because the few in the committee room will want to phone their team when you arrive and you'll then have to wait until some particularly loyal supporter gets back to see you. On the other hand, if you give them a time and stick to it, all the volunteers may enjoy a special thank you from their candidate, perhaps with a group photograph. (Photographs taken on the day can make a good collage for the wall in the constituency office.) If you're organised, it will only take 10 minutes out of the work on the day for each team. If you take refreshments round to each committee room, be consistent and don't discourage them from knocking up any more than you can help. Remember, though, that if you take refreshments for one election, you'll need to do it for every one after that.

Securing a ticket for the count

Whatever you do during election day, you should plan to attend the count of the votes and the declaration of the result. As the spouse or partner of the candidate, you are entitled to a ticket, but make sure one is actually obtained for you. These are needed by every person attending and are in limited supply. Without it, you will probably not be allowed in.

Time to regroup before the declaration of the result

Unless the election count is going to be very swift (which is only likely if the constituency is urban, with short distances for the ballot boxes to travel, or if the electorate is very small) there will probably be a long time between close of poll and declaration of the result. Going home for a good meal, a bath and a change of clothes is a positive choice, irrespective of whether your politician expects to win or lose. It's a good idea, though, to make sure there's someone at the count, usually the agent, who can telephone if it looks as if the result is going to be declared earlier than you anticipated.

> ❝ Learn what the scrutineers are doing on election night and lend a hand. It's hard to hang round with no purpose all night without looking bored, especially when photographers are present. ❞

Scrutinising the counting of the votes

If you want to make yourself useful at the count, you could volunteer to be a scrutineer. This involves watching the people doing the counting from across the counting table while they count the votes into piles of 10, 100, 1000 and so forth. (If yours is a constituency where the vote is counted electronically, this may not be an option.) Get an experienced scrutineer to explain what to watch for and what to do if you think you spot a discrepancy. It can be hugely satisfying if you spot one of your politician's votes being put into the wrong pile and you get it put right. You must not touch any of the ballot papers: you just speak up. Be wary of getting into acrimonious discussion with people from other political parties while doing this: passions and tempers often run high.

Photographers at the count

At the count, there are likely to be photographers taking pictures during the evening and there may even be film or television cameras. You need to look smart and remain courteous and friendly towards the opposition, whether your politi-

cian is winning or losing. If you are likely to get upset because things are going badly, check your face from time to time to make sure make up has not run (if you wear it) lest you be immortalised like that.

Refreshments during the count

Some election counts can go on very late into the next day. You may not be able to obtain refreshments in the building, or to leave the count to buy them once you've been allowed in, so it's a good idea to take supplies of tea, coffee, biscuits and sweets to help your team get through the long hours. Younger supporters attending their first count are often very grateful for this thought. Your politician needs to look as fresh as possible for the declaration, since that is when most of the photographs will be taken which will appear later on in the local papers.

On display on the platform?

Make sure you know in advance whether you're expected to go up on a platform or special area with your politician for the declaration: there may not be time to discuss that when you are there. It will depend on the individual Returning Officer and can vary from election to election.

A post-election party: keeping lists

After each election, whether successful or not, it's good to have a party for everyone who helped, if you have the funds. Someone will need to keep a list of names and addresses, to make sure no one misses out on an invitation. This is usually the agent's task, but if you're the person partially responsible for collating the list, it can help you learn the names of the activists. An attendance book, signed by everyone who comes to the association office to help, during the weeks leading up to the election, is also a very helpful tool, if you encourage them to write in capitals and to include full addresses.

At Westminster: the MP

Facilities for the spouse or partner at Westminster

Obtain a copy of the latest issue of 'Facilities for Members' Spouses and Partners" produced by the Sergeant at Arms for the up to date arrangements. You should obtain a photo pass, which will allow you into the Houses of Parliament and the various office buildings, and which lasts until the next election. To do this, you must go to the relevant office in the Commons with the MP. The officials take your photograph for the pass, so you may want to ensure you look your best that day. It has to be said that the facilities at the House are not particularly family or child friendly, but they are a useful base in London. The Family Room, near Central Lobby, is a good place to put your feet up and watch TV, while waiting for your politician. You can join a number of Westminster groups, the Parliamentary choir etc. For the more active, work out programmes can be followed at the Gymnasium.

Watching debates

If you have access to the Parliamentary Channel on TV at home, you can follow debates and select committee proceedings in comfort. This allows you to find out whether debates and votes are still continuing or the House has risen for the evening. Alternatively, you can usually arrange to view such proceedings in person. (Tickets are required in advance for popular events such as the Opening of Parliament.)

Know your MP's Whip

Your MP will have been assigned a Whip, another MP who is responsible for ensuring the vote is 'whipped in'. They will be in contact with the MP on a regular basis and expect to know any difficulties of any nature the MP may be facing. You may find it useful to meet them, but in any case your politician may think it a good idea to give you contact numbers (home, office, mobile) for them and the Chief Whip. This is really useful if there is an emergency when you can't first talk to the MP, such as the MP's sudden illness, an accident or a drama involving the press.

Should you work for the MP?

Many spouses and partners work for their politician as secretary or personal assistant, often at Westminster, sometimes in the constituency.

If you have the skills for that job and you feel able to work with the politician as well as living with them, then it may be a good choice. If your politician is successful and needs to spend more and more time involved in politics, then you can enjoy being part of the team, rather than feeling left behind. You will see more of the politician and gain great insight into their work. You'll also be better informed about what's going on in the constituency and who all the people are. The advice, if you are considering taking on this work, is to be quite sure it's what you want to do, rather than just to drift into it. It might help to talk to others already performing the role, since the sophistications of current office technology do require considerable expertise beyond a mere capacity to be organised. If electoral defeat strikes, remember that both of you will be out of work at the same time, and that can be particularly detrimental to the immediate family finances.

Being diplomatic with other secretaries at Westminster

If you work as the secretary or personal assistant, you will come into contact with other parliamentary secretaries, most of whom will be professional secretaries. It will not help your popularity within that tightly knit community if you boast about the grand engagements you undertake as a spouse or partner, or repeat things which have been said in private.

Working for the MP from home

If the work you do for the MP is fitted in around children or other responsibilities at home where it's not directly observed by others, it's vital to have a clear job description and to keep complete time sheets. You may start out by planning to work purely 9 to 5, but it's easy for that to slip since the politician's job is never 9 to 5. They may need to talk about office matters over breakfast or in the evening: indeed, sometimes that's the only time you get to see them. They may think, since you're both working for the same cause, that you won't mind working the sort of hours which an unrelated employee would decline. If the office is also your home, you can easily do this if you want to, but home life and office life can get very muddled if you don't draw firm dividing lines. For example, you need to consider how you'll fit in your role as spouse or partner with also being an employee. If you attend a function with the politician during the day, leaving the office unmanned, you may feel you need to work in the evening to justify your salary. Children may have critical comments if political work always seems to come first. Having other office staff around for some of the time can help avoid loneliness and share the more burdensome telephone calls, but if other employees work in your home because that is also the office, you need to consider how to separate out their working space and facilities so you retain your privacy when the whole family is at home.

Being friendly with your MP's staff

If you are not working for the politician, get to know the people in their Westminster and constituency offices well. It is they who make the MP's political life run smoothly, answering the telephone, organising the diary and making sure you know what arrangements have been made. Do not burden them with your own difficulties, however well you get on with them, but do find out how the system works. Some spouses or partners will make a point of remembering staff birthdays, others just buy presents at Christmas. Depending on the seniority of the politician, there may be other staff, such as a driver or researcher to consider, too.

Lines of contact with the MP during the day

It's helpful to arrange with your politician how you can contact them swiftly during the day. Perhaps agree that you'll be put straight through to them if you phone in during the day and they are in their office. Text messages are an easy way of sending personal messages to them, which need not disrupt a meeting. Voicemail on a mobile phone can be left provided you are sure the voice-mailbox is secure. Be aware that any messages you send via the paging systems or parliamentary e-mail go through a central server, with possible delays and lack of privacy. Some MPs do not deal with their own e-mails, but have them filtered by members of staff.

The master diary

Unless you have an extremely organised and efficient politician, it's best to have one master diary. Without that, double bookings and recriminations will dog your life. Some spouses and partners remain in charge of the diary themselves – in which case they have to be available all the time to deal with it (but that way, you're more likely to keep Sundays or specific weekends free). Alternatively, the diary is kept in the Westminster office. If you are going to make this latter system work, you must make sure you pass to the person keeping the diary full details of all the events you wish the MP to attend. School sports days and plays may otherwise be missed unintentionally. It is seldom sufficient to have told the MP over breakfast, if you did not see them write the information down. Some people use an electronic master diary which can be accessed from the Internet or on a black-berry. That allows easy remote access, but requires some discipline about who is allowed to make decisions about diary clashes and competing events.

Diary discipline

Friends and relations may well raise an eyebrow if you claim you cannot book the family up for family events without checking with the master diary, but it's a sensible discipline and should avoid the disappointment of clashes. Another way of dealing with time management is to have regular 'diary reconciliation' discussions, where you and the politician go through your respective diaries and make plans accordingly. This is only likely to work if the diary for one of you is relatively flexible. You may find it helpful to be given a print out of the MP's expected diary in advance each week, and to have an occasional long term warning list of the events which you are invited to attend in the future.

Thank you letters

Be sure you and the politician are clear about who is going to write a thank-you letter after any event. Otherwise you may find, a month later, that neither of you has done so. (It's generally the case that a letter from you is regarded as second best, but if you enjoy writing letters and can make them special, it may enhance the recipient's pleasure.)

Christmas cards

If the politician decides to send Christmas cards to activists, you may wish to help with the task by compiling lists of names and addresses. The association's list of branch and constituency officers will be a useful starting point. Check that it's up to date. The local councillors will also be on lists, with contact addresses. Beyond that, you should consult carefully with the politician about who else ought to be included, paying special attention to anyone who may have moved or died in the course of the past year. Don't just rely on last year's list.

Data protection

If you are keeping lists of names and addresses on a personal computer, even for something as simple as a Christmas card list, you may need to consider Data Protection Registration, to stay within the law. The association is likely to be covered, but that will not extend to you if you are working on a computer outside the office. You may already be registered in your own right because of your own job: but check that your registration includes political activities. At present registration costs £35 per year, irrespective of the number of categories of data included.

Houses of Parliament presents

A wide range of Parliamentary goods can be bought at the House of Commons shop, and a more limited range in Portcullis House. There is also a mail order service for MPs. Most spouses and partners find that wider family members and friends enjoy receiving these as presents in the first year after election, but enthusiasm then rather tails off. They remain popular for special occasions and celebrations. Tins of Humbugs and Fudge are favourites.

Publicity and Privacy

The delicate balance between publicity and intrusion

Politicians thrive on fame in their political endeavours, but also seek to avoid ridicule and bad publicity. Frequently the desire for recognition clashes with keeping their personal and family life private. It sometimes feels as if journalists regard any MP as a sufficient celebrity to justify intrusion. The higher the profile of your politician, the more persistent the interest likely to be shown, but since every politician is a minor celebrity in their own constituency, no one is immune. There are delicate balances to be achieved in this area. Some spouses and partners just shun the limelight, but can then find themselves portrayed in the media in a one-dimensional way, if they've not taken steps to present their characters as they would wish. There are also problems when the politician's partner has a high profile job, which is itself the subject of media comment. It will be especially important to make it clear that the two parties to the relationship are distinct individuals, and it may require more scrupulous avoidance of comment on the other's territory.

What to put on the website

Discuss with the politician how much detail concerning yourself and any children should be displayed on constituency or party websites. This includes names, ages, your work, schools attended and home address. Many politicians start out by providing copious detail, to prove to their electorate what normal family lives they lead. But the more information you give, the less you can complain if it is used in the public domain if something goes wrong in the lives of any family member. A quick review of the current websites reveals that most MPs put much more personal information on their constituency websites than on the party website, but it is all still there on the Net. Remember that absolutely anyone may look at your website entries and may print them out. Amusing anecdotes which seemed suitable at one period of your life for a particular coterie of friends can be wilfully misunderstood when taken out of context, and may turn out to be hugely embarrassing later on.

Photographs on websites

Family pictures on the website are sometimes downloaded and reprinted in newspapers. Newspapers tend not to check about copyright before doing this. They are obliged to pay a fee to the photographer, if challenged, but by then the photograph may have been printed and misused.

Putting yourself in the public domain

There may be times when you will be encouraged by the politician, or the party, to speak to a journalist about yourself or your life on the periphery of politics. Think about it carefully and decline politely unless you enjoy living a little dangerously and can cope with possible ridicule. Your relationship with your politician is none of the public's business unless you yourself put that material in the public domain. If you decide to do that, make sure the journalist is clear that you are speaking for yourself, not on behalf of the politician. Unless you are writing the piece or have been given a right to veto the content, remember you have no control over how the material is presented to public gaze. It is surprising how many inaccuracies can creep into the simplest piece, even when it is based on an uncritical, clear interview. Very often, too, the journalist will have no control over the layout or the wording of the headline of the piece. Unless you are ready for these problems, you may be put off getting involved again, after just one such exercise, which can be a shame. In many cases, this sort of exercise can be a powerful presentational tool for your politician, but it's not for the faint hearted.

Talking to journalists who telephone

Sometimes you may answer the telephone to a journalist who wants your politician to comment on an issue. However friendly the journalist, don't be led into guessing what the politician might say, even if you think you know what their answer would be. Just take the number and say the politician will call them when they can. Be particularly vigilant about saying something off hand to a journalist during an election campaign, even an apparently friendly one. The chances are it will be written up as if your politician had themselves given the quote, rather than you.

Keeping children out of the spotlight

If you are anxious about keeping your children's lives private, you should make it clear to the editor of the local paper at the outset that you don't wish your children's pictures to appear. If you take that stance, then you would also need to be consistent and not allow constituents or other photographers to take group photographs of you with your children. Very small children may not mind being named, but as they get older, children can be acutely embarrassed and young adults may prefer to remain anonymous, so they can lead their own lives. If something goes wrong in the life of a young adult, which has no real bearing on the politician parent, it is hugely unfair to both the offspring and the politician if the problem is made public just because the family life of the politician has previously been in the public eye.

> ❝ None of us knows what is going to happen later in life and the prospect of the press coming back and saying 'Well, you were happy enough to use your children to get elected, so you can't complain if we run this story about your son/daughter now' is too horrible to contemplate. ❞

Coping with personal attacks

Personal political attacks can come at any time and seem to be part of certain types of campaigning style. They are especially common during election campaigns, particularly in marginal seats, where opposition parties very frequently resort to attacking the politician personally through their family or lifestyle. Attacks may also occur within the party, particularly if your politician has been successful in some endeavour, and others are jealous. Outright lies are relatively easy to deal with, but sometimes people dredge up and misconstrue some long distant incident in the politician's history. The advice, which is not easy to follow, is to ignore the attack and just to move on without comment or retaliation. The more high profile and successful the politician becomes, the greater the likelihood that other people will indulge in this sort of attack, and the thicker the skin you, personally, are going to need to develop. Since it is probably the case that few politicians have done nothing risible or embarrassing or stupid in their past history, you're probably going to need to learn to laugh off such slurs. Brooding on the attacks will just make you a miserable person and will help no one but your politician's detractors.

The likelihood of press intrusion

Sadly, it's highly likely, at some stage during the political career of your politician, that a journalist will attempt to intrude into your lives. Sometimes the story being pursued will be accurate, but it can just as easily be partially or wholly inaccurate. Cases of mistaken identity, especially if your politician has a name easily muddled with someone else, are very common if journalists are lax in checking sources. Don't assume such intrusion is a rare occurrence or that it won't ever happen to you. Without warning, you may find yourself confronted on your doorstep, in the street or at your workplace, by a journalist

asking you questions about your politician. The chances are you won't have any idea whether what they're saying is true or not. Anticipating this sort of event is essential, even if you are totally convinced of your politician's irreproachable character, because you won't have the luxury of thinking time if it occurs. It's a good idea to have a standard response ready to tide you over: one that's slightly more exciting than saying "No comment" and rushing away. Keep in mind that the journalist may simply be trying to stand up a vague piece of malicious gossip, fed to them by some disgruntled person. They may be confronting you with all sorts of lies, just to see whether they get a reaction from you.

> ❝ The Westminster lobby journalists are less likely to 'do you over' if they know you personally and have sat round your kitchen table. Mind you, we've had to sue once, and it was pretty hideous, even though we won. ❞

Alert neighbours and friends to possible tactics

Journalists may try the same trick of trying to stand up a story with members of your respective families or close friends or neighbours. Even an unconsidered word in response may be misconstrued and turned into a 'story'. If you're out of the house or don't answer the door, the journalist may knock on your neighbours' doors to see whether they can get information from them. If you are on good terms with your neighbours, let them know about this tactic, so they're not taken by surprise.

> ❝ It's very easy for an individual who is not used to media intrusion to be caught off guard and an innocent word can unwittingly add to the difficulty of the situation. ❞

Journalists in parked cars

Journalists or photographers sometimes wait in parked cars near your home if they don't get an immediate response. The length of time they are prepared to wait will usually depend on their publication deadline and on whether there are parking restrictions in place. Taking their car registration number or photographing them may not especially unnerve them, but it can give you a sense of control, and you'll have evidence for use in a complaint against their news organisation. A friendly neighbour, involved in Neighbourhood Watch, might also enjoy going out to challenge someone loitering suspiciously.

The journalist with two photographers

If the journalist has two photographers with them, don't assume they're from different news organisations. Their expectation may well be that you'll attempt to grab one of the cameras to prevent a picture being taken, and that the other photographer will snap that being done, so giving them a 'story' entirely independent of whatever it was they were going to approach you about.

How to respond to a journalist's approach

The following ideas may be a useful guide when dealing with a single journalist, although they are probably a counsel of perfection.

a   Don't assume there's any truth in what's being said to you and try not to react or make any comment on it at all.

b   If you are able to record the conversation on a mobile phone or other device, do so.

c   Ask them for a contact telephone number and for the name of their immediate editor.

d   Ask your own questions: taking careful notes of the journalist's name, news organisation, and the precise terms of what is being put to you.

e   If what they say keeps changing, try to get each of the variants down on paper.

f   If they offer you anything in a brown envelope, accept it, but don't open the envelope in front of them.

g   Refer them to the politician, if appropriate, by giving them the telephone number of the office.

h   If you have a camera phone, take a picture of them.

i   Most difficult, quell any hot flush of rising panic (it's quite possible nothing dreadful is about to break over your head); explain you do not wish to speak to them and that they should not contact you again. Smile and walk away, or shut the door.

j   If the journalist persists, point out that the Press Complaints Commission's Code of Practice requires journalists not to continue to contact you if you've told them to desist. Tell them you're saying the same to all other journalists.

k   Pin/stick a note to your front door, saying you don't wish to speak to journalists and don't wish to be disturbed. Change your answer machine message to say the same thing.

Who to contact after an approach

As soon as you can after any such approach by a journalist, make careful notes of everything said and done. If you don't, a flurry of events may cause you to forget important details or to get events out of order. Talk to your politician about it. They will probably want you to speak to someone who has experience of dealing with the press. The Whips Office is one possibility. Another is the Press Complaints Commission: (they have a 24 hour advice line – 07659 152656). Tell them the full and unvarnished truth. Don't bottle it up, or try to deal with the problem on your own, or assume it'll just go away if you ignore it. It's a good idea not to telephone the journalist or the editor, whatever you may have said to them (but if you do, remember they'll be recording your call and may use anything you say, quite possibly out of context.) Threats to take legal action to prevent publication are more effective when issued through the party or lawyers. Keep careful records of any repeated attempts to contact you and make a complaint to the PCC about it (complaints@pcc.org.uk).

The value of avoiding publication

It's best to do all you can to defuse any 'story'. Once something, however untrue or inaccurate, has appeared in the media, particularly in national newspapers, it's very difficult to correct the error in a way which obliterates its effect. News gathering search engines will still pick up the original reference, but may not include the subsequent correction or retraction. Family, friends and neighbours need to be encouraged to take the same course. Even the receipt of substantial libel damages is seldom sufficient compensation and seems to be regarded as an occupational hazard by some journalists.

What to do in a news frenzy

If, despite those efforts, your politician has become the subject of a news frenzy, you may find journalists and photographers encamped outside your house for days on end. What they are hoping to get are photographs or film of people involved in their 'story', or some new comment. A closed front door is seldom newsworthy for more than one news cycle. Offering cups of tea to those barricading your home is a traditional way of allowing the politician to be photographed in an informal way during the frenzy. It does, however, suggest you regard your persecutors as fellow human beings, perhaps in on some joke. Keep on keeping notes of everything. Take photographs of anything you regard as intrusive on your life. A video camera or video phone is even more helpful, if you need to make a complaint about journalists' behaviour, later on.

Keeping children private during a news frenzy

Practical considerations may mean you and your children have to pass encamped journalists to go about your normal life. Explain things to the children before you go out, so they are not too upset. Attempt to keep an enigmatic smile on your face. Your children are entitled to special protection from newspaper journalists under the Press Complaints Commission's Code of Conduct. Clause 6 makes it clear, for example, that young people should be free to complete their time at school without unnecessary intrusion, and that editors must not use the fame, notoriety or position of a parent as sole justification for publishing details about a child's private life. A child under 16 must not be interviewed or photographed on issues involving their own or another child's welfare without the consent of their parent. (These provisions do not apply to broadcast journalists in the same way, but the PCC will forward complaints to broadcasting organisations who will consider whether action is appropriate, usually on the same basis.)

Don't brood on a news frenzy

If you find yourself becoming especially incensed at things written about your politician, your children or yourself, it may be a good idea to stop reading those things and to avoid television or radio news for the duration of the frenzy. You will be better able to function in a supportive role if you are not indignantly seething. Try, too, not to become obsessed about minor points of inaccuracy in the reporting, or you will lose focus.

The risks of putting your side of a story

There may be some occasions when you feel it would be useful to give an interview or speak out, or to allow a relative or friend to speak out on your behalf. A journalist may, for instance, suggest you should tell your side of the 'story', to correct the inaccuracies other journalists have already printed. Whatever the state of your emotions, the advice is: don't do it. You will just give an added twist to a story with otherwise dying interest, and will regret it later. If in doubt about the best course of action, buy some of the tabloid Sunday papers and see the way they write about other people in your position. Is that how you want to be portrayed?

Appreciating the transience of notoriety

Whatever the nature of the media interest, the caravan usually moves on, and other stories grip the press imagination. Your life, however, will probably never be quite the same again. Friends may make innocent or pointed comments about what has happened. You may not be able to face particular individuals who passed on malicious gossip, or the journalists who wrote it up, without wanting to commit acts of violence. There is a possibility you may sense, rightly or wrongly, that others are laughing at the situation. If you talk to other people who have been through the same mangle, you may be surprised how many have felt just the same. This can help you rebuild your own esteem, and put the episode in context. It's important you carry out that process rather than just bottling it up or brushing it aside. Regaining a healthy perception of the lack of long term importance of the story will enable you to move on and stop you feeling so bruised.

Legal advice on defamation

If you really think you've been defamed, seek and accept competent legal advice before taking any action. If you complain unsuccessfully, you may just revive the original story unnecessarily and so cause greater misery for all, as well as putting yourself to excessive legal expense.

Personal organisation

Your political views are your own

Some spouses or partners have their own strongly held political views. While such opinions may be similar to those of the politician, they are unlikely to be identical. It's wise to be clear you're not speaking for the politician when you express your own views, not just when speaking to journalists or at party events, but even when chatting to friends. This is particularly the case if you profoundly disagree with your politician on an individual issue.

> ❝ It's important to have something outside of politics that cushions you. ❞

Following your own career

It has always seemed to be accepted that male spouses and partners will have their own independent work or career. It was less common until recent years for female spouses and partners to be similarly engaged. In some places there is still a lack of appreciation that the job of a spouse or partner may well be more than just being a spouse, parent or partner. A woman who retains her own surname, for example, may have to put up with being criticised for being a 'radical feminist'. The advice is always to be patient with such different expectations.

The advantages of self-employment or flexible working

Spouses and partners who are self employed have a relatively easier time of fitting in party and constituency events, particularly if they can choose their own hours. It may be, as well, that they can skew their work efforts so that they're more available, perhaps during an election period, or when children need support through exams and the politician cannot escape parliamentary duties.

> **It's OK to have your own career and not be a political acolyte**

Pursuing your own projects and goals

However closely you associate yourself with the candidate or MP, as a secretary, personal assistant or loyal supporter, it is widely said to be a bad idea to immerse yourself in their politics to the exclusion of everything else. Develop separate interests and always have a personal project on the go. It will act as a cushion against the all too pervasive impact of politics. A political spouse or partner who's too ambitious for their politician can be a real hindrance to them. It's widely recommended you should not make your politician's success your sole project. It's fashionable to talk about achieving a work-life balance, but the political spouse or partner has the added dimension of a work-life-politics balance. The project might be anything from the all consuming to the transient. It might be something intellectual, or relate to your own work, or to your children's interests, or be just a hobby. Encouraging the politician to take up their own project, separate from politics, may also be helpful. People frequently automatically assume, since they see you in a political context, that all you want to talk about is politics. If they're wrong about that, having a project gives you something unusual to talk about, and means they might see you in a different light as more of an independent being.

❝ It's great for the spouse's morale to have an intellectual, or fun, or creative project on the go like a 19th century vicar, with an interest in nature keeping rainfall charts which have helped later with climate understanding.❞

The difficulty of retaining friends outside politics

Once the politician is seriously engaged in the fray of election fighting, and especially after they're elected, there's a risk your previous social life will grind to a halt (unless you only ever socialised with other politicians and their families). Your old friends will think you've become too grand for them when you keep turning down invitations. You need to find some way of explaining to them – without seeking an excess of sympathy – that most evenings are taken up with political meetings and branch events. You need to explain – again, without sounding too grand – that the politician really is booked up weeks or months in advance and that they need to think a long time ahead if they want to see you both.

Ways of keeping in touch with old friends

That said, it's unwise to cut yourself off completely from your old friends. They're the ones you will want to fall back on, if political disaster strikes or your relationship with the politician comes to an end. You won't want to find your friends have melted away in the way that some of your political friends will fade, if you become 'unimportant'. Consider holding a big party every now and then for them all, and keep in touch with Christmas cards, letters, calls and e-mails. If the politician is busy, why not accept an invitation on your own: you don't always have to go as a couple.

Involvement with charities

Some people erroneously assume that all politicians are wealthy and that consequently you can support every charity and join every local interest organisation. They also assume that all spouses and partners have sufficient spare time to become heavily involved in many different charities. They can be quite indignant if you refuse when they ask you to join. If you already have a particular charity which you support, stick to it. Others in the constituency will have their own favourite charities and may try to persuade you to join them. You'll soon find there are dozens and dozens of possible contenders for your energies. Someone particularly keen may sign you up to theirs at an early stage, only for you to discover something else might have been a more appropriate choice for you. While most charities are very deserving, you simply cannot support everything financially or in terms of the time involved. It may be a good idea to choose one charity, perhaps with a special connection to your family, or a set of local charities, that you always support. That way you can satisfy those who expect people in public life to be philanthropic, while keeping some control of the calls on your time and money beyond politics.

National fund raising

As a political spouse or partner you may be invited to help with national party fund raising efforts. This can be a useful way of meeting other spouses and partners, but it can also be time and money intensive. At the least, you may be expected to persuade a group of personal friends to make significant financial contributions to a party, dinner or ball, by collecting together a table. Generating advertising and seeking donations of prizes are also sometimes expected. If you have a flair for such organisation, you will be welcomed with open arms.

> ❝ The annual House of Lords vs House of Commons Tug-of-War is a fun thing to be involved with and is cross-party, so you get to meet lots of other spouses and partners. ❞

Take advice on personal security

Take advice from the local police force about the security of your property, put their advice into action, and notify them if you have any specific concerns. They'll be aware that any politician can be a target for extremists or lunatics and will have experience at assessing the level of any particular risk. Don't assume your politician is so insignificant that they won't be targeted.

Use a shredder

A shredder is a good investment, provided you do get into the habit of shredding all personal papers. Not only will it deter dustbin marauders, but it will help to prevent general identity theft and similar frauds. Recycling of shredded paper is environmentally sound, too.

Take messages rather than giving out information

If anyone contacts you, particularly by phone, and will not give their name and return telephone number, be wary of giving out any information. Be especially careful about giving them information about the politician's whereabouts or schedule. You may be speaking to a member of an opposing political party or an unfriendly journalist who wants to make mischief. It's far safer, if you don't personally know the caller, to offer to take a message and a return telephone number.

The vulnerability of mobile phones

Be aware, if you haven't changed the security code for your mobile phone voice-mailbox, that it's possible for other people to listen to your voice-mail and even to delete messages. All they need do is telephone your number while your phone is not switched on, key in the factory security code, and then listen to any messages that may be there. If your mobile phone mysteriously rings once without anyone apparently being there, it may be someone or an automatic dialling system trying to break into your box. Listening to messages on voice-mails is one of the ways that journalists and opposing politicians gain sensitive information about your plans and arrangements. Change the code !

The usefulness of camera/video phones

If you are buying a new mobile phone, get one that can take photographs and videos. There are often situations when you'd love to be able to record a political moment and don't have a conventional camera with you.

Put a confidentiality clause in an employment contract

Many families are able to perform the child care juggling exercise without needing to employ any carers. Sometimes a grandparent is available, or a parent's time is sufficiently flexible to fit around school and political activities. For others, though, child care has to be paid for. Consider a confidentiality clause when choosing someone to help with your children, or around the home. It's highly unlikely you will employ someone who would wish to sell details of the dullness of your home life to the newspapers, but it's always comforting to know you have a confidentiality clause in any employment contract. Keep in mind, that if they have friends or relatives to stay in your home, the confidentiality clause will not cover those people.

Personal views of employees

The private political views of an employee are seldom something you'll ask about or that will impinge on you. But if you don't make it clear in advance that they're going to be working for a politician or prospective politician, it may not be apparent to them that you would take a dim view of your children being taught something incompatible with your own beliefs: whether on such topics as education, hunting or monetary policy. This applies to all sorts of things beyond politics, as well:

religion, vegetarianism and the anthropomorphizing of animals; and it emphasises the importance of carefully interviewing anyone you employ for yourself and not relying upon an agency to do the sifting for you. This is all the more important if the person is going to live in your home and perhaps have sole charge of your children, especially during election periods.

Paying tax and national insurance for employees

The responsibility for discovering whether your household needs to pay the tax and National Insurance contributions of an employee will probably fall on you. Generally speaking, if you are the workers' only employer and their earnings are above a specific limit, then you will need to pay them a net wage and to account to the Revenue for income tax and NI. Other types of workers, such as child minders, cleaners and gardeners, who have many customers, will generally be self-employed and you will not need to account for tax. You do need to check, because the rules and limits change from time to time. If you employ someone and do not properly account for tax and NI, then it could be damaging to the politician's career, even if the politician left all those domestic arrangements to you. There are specialist accountants who, for a modest annual fee, provide a payroll service for such employees, giving you clear evidence (should it ever be needed) that you have paid all that was required.

Considerations when employing carers from abroad

If an employee is someone who comes from abroad, then it is wise to satisfy yourself that they are working in the UK legally. If they are from outside the EU they can show you their entry visa. If they don't want you to have a copy of their documentation, think twice about employing them. Children can become desperately fond of a carer who is under a visa obligation to return home on a specific date. Don't let their distress tempt you to try to bend the rules or to ask favours from the politician, even though you will hear anecdotes of dispensations granted to other families. Your children will learn the need to keep to the rules and they can always be encouraged to keep in touch with the carer who has gone home by e-mail etc.

Employees during election campaigns

If an employee is likely to be working for you during an election, you need to make sure they appreciate that life may be more than usually chaotic at that time. Try to agree contingency plans from the outset, since you don't want to have to organise new child care in the middle of

113

an unexpected election campaign, if someone has walked out because they were being asked to work different hours to the times agreed in advance.

Special considerations for a second spouse or partner

Where you are not the first spouse or partner of your politician known to the constituency, you may find it useful to agree a simple form of words with your politician about their previous relationship. Presenting a coherent front may help neutralise residual hostility or upset in the association. A former spouse who died is likely to be remembered with great fondness and you may always feel you are being adversely compared with the memory of a paragon. It's better not to attempt to compete, but to make it clear that you're bringing your own different style to the role. If you're the new spouse or partner of a sitting MP, you may find you need to undergo a rapid learning curve to keep up with their life. People will assume you know what is expected and you may therefore not like to ask. It's useful to talk to others who've had a similar experience about how they coped. It has been suggested there should be a mentoring scheme for anyone in this position, although that's only arranged informally, at present. Having someone on the end of a phone to answer questions and to give advice might make all the difference.

The advantages of being public about illness

If serious illness strikes the politician, or you, or a child, it can be extremely difficult to know whether it's a good idea to be public about the problem. Talk to the MP's whip, or the Chief Whip if the politician is not available. They have heard it all before, and will give good advice. Sometimes the need to decide is taken away from you because it's obvious to all that something has occurred. The politician may have no choice but to explain why they are distracted or taking time away from the fray. If you are public about the difficulties, you may discover a supportive network you never knew existed of people and families who have been touched by the same illness. Sometimes they can put you in touch with experts or therapies that have worked for them. Sometimes, being cared about and thought about can, in itself, be therapeutic.

The disadvantages of being public about illness

Being public about a short lived illness may leave the sufferer permanently labelled as the person who suffered from that particular illness, long after they have been completely cured. Sometimes that can lead to others regarding the individual as weakened or potentially unreliable: particularly tricky for the politician. It can also be very wearing to have even the most sympathetic of enquiries about your health repeated by everyone you meet.

Minor illnesses can also generate their own problems. Discourage the politician from explaining away your absence from a particular event with the easy excuse that you're unwell, especially if that's not the full reason. You'll be the subject of intrusive questions for weeks after (or interested speculation, if you are female and of child-bearing age).

Strategies for dealing with political failure

Everything that could happen to your politician has already happened to someone else and there's bound to be another political spouse or partner who can act as a shoulder to cry on, if failure strikes. 'The Other Half' (formerly known as Conservative Parliamentary Wives) is a good starting point if you want confidential help from colleagues. The Parliamentary Wives' Christian Fellowship, too. Lost elections; lost jobs; lost chances; lost reputations; lost relationships: nothing is new. Coming to terms with the sheer unfairness of apparently arbitrary political decisions is often the most difficult. There is undoubtedly life after such disasters, provided you seek it out, just as others have done before you.

> It's very important to identify some kindred spirits so that when the going gets tough you can go and feel comfortable with them.

Strategies for dealing with political success

Political success can bring its own complications, with your politician becoming more and more involved in other activities beyond the family circle. If you're not working for your politician, it's easy to feel excluded. Don't nag, but instead make a special effort within the more limited time you have together. The tyranny of the pager, mobile phone or blackberry mean that even on holiday it's possible for the politician to

be contacted for a comment on an issue or to deal with a crisis. There's little point fighting against this. Put a cover over their meal, be prepared for a change of plans and joke about it with the children. Throwing the offending communication device in the pool is probably unhelpful, if tempting. Turning it off is the better strategy.

117

Enjoy being a political spouse or partner

The conclusion to this book (which may surprise you if you've read it all) is that if you're ready for the difficulties of political life, you're more likely to overcome them and carve out a highly enjoyable existence as a political spouse or partner. You'll make lasting friends in the political world. You'll meet a wide range of people. You might travel to unexpected places. You'll share the ups and downs of political life and have the vicarious pleasure of being close to the centre of power, without the responsibility.

There's a lot you can enjoy in that.

Garden Design

teNeues

Imprint

Produced by fusion publishing GmbH, Stuttgart . Los Angeles   www.fusion-publishing.com

Editorial team:
Haike Falkenberg (Editor + texts)
Hanna Martin, Anne-Kathrin Meier (Editorial coordination)
Kerstin Graf, Hanna Martin (Layout)
Jan Hausberg, Anke Scholz (Prepress + imaging)
Alphagriese Fachübersetzungen, Düsseldorf (Translations)
Dr. Suzanne Kirkbright, Artes Translations, UK (Copy Editing)

Cover photo (location): Patrizia Pozzi (Small Green Rooms)

Back cover photos from top to bottom (location): Claas Dreppenstedt (Carlebach Park), Marion Brenner (Hillsborough Residence), H.G. Esch, Hennef (Lufthansa Aviation Center), Vladimir Sitta (Garden of Ghosts), David Cook (TDCCBR)

Introduction photos (page, location): Daici Ano (page 11, Lotus House), Stefan Behnisch (page 4, TDCCBR), Marion Brenner (page 3, Hillsborough Residence), Anthony Charlesworth (page 5, Red Garden), Stephen Jerrom (page 10, Vego Garden), Minao Tabata (page 6, Rensho.ji; page 7, Opus Arisugawa Terrace), Brian Tichenor (page 9, Beverly Hills Pool House), courtesy Bet Figueras (page 8, Masia in Emporda)

Published by teNeues Publishing Group

teNeues Verlag GmbH + Co. KG
Am Selder 37
47906 Kempen, Germany
Tel.: 0049-(0)2152-916-0
Fax: 0049-(0)2152-916-111
E-mail: books@teneues.de

teNeues Publishing Company
16 West 22nd Street
New York, NY 10010, USA
Tel.: 001-212-627-9090
Fax: 001-212-627-9511

teNeues Publishing UK Ltd.
P.O. Box 402
West Byfleet
KT14 7ZF, Great Britain
Tel.: 0044-1932-403509
Fax: 0044-1932-403514

teNeues France S.A.R.L.
93, rue Bannier
45000 Orléans, France
Tel.: 0033-2-38541071
Fax: 0033-2-38625340

Press department: arehn@teneues.de
Tel.: 0049-(0)2152-916-202

www.teneues.com

ISBN: 978-3-8327-9228-2

© 2008 teNeues Verlag GmbH + Co. KG, Kempen

Second Edition

Printed in Italy

Bibliographic information published by Die Deutsche Bibliothek.
Die Deutsche Bibliothek lists this publication in the Deutsche Nationalbibliografie; detailed bibliographic data is available in the Internet at http://dnb.ddb.de.

Introduction 6

Introduction

GARDEN DESIGN today involves gardens in all shapes and sizes designed and created by landscape architects, garden designers, architects or artists. The success of a project doesn't depend on the size, location or environment of the property in question. Nor does it depend on whether the property is designated for private, commercial or public use or on the budget made available for initiating and maintaining the project. Rather, it depends on the close cooperation between the garden designer, the architect of the structure involved and the owner of the property to ensure that the interior design of the living space is in tone with the exterior design and that it incorporates all requirements and intended forms of use.

This is the basis for designing office buildings in which perfectly arranged green areas inside improve the work climate so significantly as noticeably to reduce the number of sick days. Another factor is the significant cut in energy costs. Today, we see gardens placed in areas where we may not even expect them. Take, for example, rooftops that, once they're turned into gardens, open up new living environments and decidedly improve the quality of our living space as well as our lives. At the same time, they provide at least some counterbalance to the negative effect of sealing off too much space. In doing so, they do justice to another important aspect: the respectful approach to nature. Ideally, the concept of sustainability will be part of the equation. In other words, the idea is to utilize a natural system, capable of regenerating itself, in a way that preserves its essential features and allows its riches to regrow naturally. Cisterns for rainwater or retaining reservoirs for areas prone to heavy rainfall are integrated quite naturally into a design and artistically upgraded, so that it may take an observer a second or third glance to recognize what they are. In fact, observers may not recognize this design at all until it's expressly pointed out to them. That wouldn't be surprising and certainly no cause for dismay. Because every single design presented here has its own unique appeal and effect on the beholder. Blame it on another artifice that the masters of garden design are adept at: namely, to add a touch of mystery to all their projects.

Haike Falkenberg

Einleitung

GARDEN DESIGN heute, darunter versteht man Gärten in wirklich allen Formen und Größen, die von Landschaftsarchitekten, Gartengestaltern, Architekten oder Künstlern entworfen und realisiert werden. Dabei ist es für den Erfolg eines Projektes nicht ausschlaggebend, welche Größe, Lage oder Umgebung das Grundstück hat, ob es privat, gewerblich oder öffentlich genutzt wird, und ebensowenig wie hoch das Budget ist, das für die Einrichtung und Unterhaltung zur Verfügung steht. Vielmehr kommt es darauf an, dass der Gartendesigner eng mit dem Architekten des Gebäudes und den Grundstückseigentümern zusammenarbeitet, damit die Gestaltung der Lebensräume innen und außen Hand in Hand geht und auf die Wünsche und Nutzungsformen eingeht.

Auf dieser Grundlage entstehen unter anderem Bürogebäude, in denen durch perfekt arrangierte Grünbereiche im Inneren des Gebäudes das Arbeitsklima so entscheidend verbessert wird, dass die Zahl der Krankmeldungen spürbar zurückgeht. Des Weiteren werden die Energiekosten erheblich gesenkt. Gärten werden heute dort angelegt, wo man es manchmal vielleicht nicht vermutet. Zum Beispiel auf Dächern, die begrünt neuen Lebensraum erschließen und eine ausgesprochene Verbesserung der Wohn- und Lebensqualität darstellen. Gleichzeitig heben sie den negativen Einfluss der Flächenversiegelung zumindest teilweise wieder auf und tragen somit einem weiteren wichtigen Aspekt Rechnung: dem respektvollen Umgang mit der Natur, im idealen Fall die Berücksichtigung des Konzepts der Nachhaltigkeit. Dieses besagt, dass ein regenerierbares natürliches System so genutzt wird, dass es in seinen wesentlichen Eigenschaften erhalten bleibt und sein Bestand auf natürliche Weise nachwachsen kann. Zisternen für Regenwasser oder Rückhaltebecken für hohe Niederschlagsmengen werden ganz selbstverständlich in einen Entwurf integriert und künstlerisch aufgewertet, sodass der Betrachter vielleicht erst auf den zweiten oder dritten Blick erkennt, was dahinter steckt. Eventuell enthüllt sich ihm eine solche Konzeption auch überhaupt erst durch ausdrückliche Erklärungen, das verwundert nicht und stört noch weniger. Denn jeder einzelne der hier vorgestellten Entwürfe hat einen besonderen Reiz und seine Wirkung auf den Betrachter. Das liegt an einem weiteren Kunstgriff, den die Könner des Gartendesigns beherrschen, nämlich in jedem Projekt auch etwas Geheimnisvolles zu verbergen.

Haike Falkenberg

Introduction

Qu'est-ce qu'un GARDEN DESIGN aujourd'hui ? Le terme englobe des jardins de toutes formes et tailles conçus et créés par des architectes paysagistes, des créateurs de jardins, des architectes ou des artistes. Le facteur essentiel pour le succès d'un tel projet n'est pas la taille, l'emplacement ou l'environnement de la propriété. Ce n'est pas non plus l'usage commercial, privé ou public du jardin. Et le budget disponible pour l'installation et l'entretien ne compte pas tellement non plus. Cela dépend plutôt de la collaboration étroite entre le concepteur du jardin, l'architecte du bâtiment et le propriétaire du jardin pour que les designs des espaces de vie intérieurs et extérieurs fonctionnent bien ensemble et correspondent aux souhaits et aux types d'utilisation voulus.

C'est la base pour créer des immeubles de bureau dans lesquels le climat de travail est résolument amélioré par des espaces verts à l'intérieur de la structure, le nombre de jours de maladie diminuant ainsi de manière notable. Les coûts en énergie sont également considérablement réduits. Les jardins sont maintenant placés dans des lieux où nous ne nous attendrions pas à les voir. Par exemple, sur des toits où ils ouvrent les nouveaux habitats et représentent une amélioration visible du confort et de la qualité de vie. Parallèlement, ils inversent au moins en partie l'effet négatif des surfaces enduites. Ils prennent donc en considération un autre aspect plus important : l'approche respectueuse de la nature. Ainsi, un système naturel régénérable est utilisé de manière à préserver les traits essentiels, permettant à la végétation de pousser dans un environnement encore naturel. Des citernes ou des réservoirs pour collecter l'eau de pluie, selon les quantités, sont intégrés assez naturellement dans le design. Leur esthétique est ensuite revue de manière à ce que l'observateur ait besoin de regarder une deuxième ou une troisième fois pour les identifier. Un tel concept ne peut se révéler au spectateur qu'après une explication explicite qui ne le surprendra pas et ne le dérangera certainement pas. Chacun des jardins présentés ici a un charme spécifique qui fait effet sur l'observateur. C'est grâce à une autre astuce que les experts du design de jardin ont appris à maîtriser : donner à chaque projet une part de mystère.

Haike Falkenberg

Introducción

GARDEN DESIGN; con este concepto se entiende hoy la idea de jardines en todas las formas y tamaños imaginables, proyectados y hechos realidad por arquitectos paisajísticos, diseñadores de jardines, arquitectos o artistas. El éxito de un proyecto no viene determinado por el tamaño, la ubicación o el entorno de un terreno, por su uso privado, comercial o público ni tampoco por el presupuesto disponible para su creación y mantenimiento. Depende más bien de la estrecha colaboración entre el diseñador del jardín, el arquitecto de la edificación y el propietario del terreno, con el fin de que la organización de los espacios vitales interiores y exteriores vaya de la mano y satisfaga los deseos y modos de aplicación.

Con este principio, se están construyendo, entre otros, edificios de oficinas en los que gracias a sus zonas verdes interiores perfectamente organizadas, la atmósfera de trabajo ha mejorado; y en tal medida, que el número de bajas por enfermedad ha disminuido de forma significativa, y se han reducido considerablemente los gastos energéticos. Hoy en día, los jardines se emplazan en lugares donde cuesta imaginárselos; por ejemplo en azoteas, en las que se crean nuevos espacios naturales y con ello mejora claramente la calidad de vida y de vivienda. Al mismo tiempo, eliminan al menos en parte la negativa influencia de la limitación de las superficies y con ello se ocupan de otro aspecto determinante: tratar de forma respetuosa a la naturaleza y, en el mejor de los casos, tener en consideración el concepto de la sostenibilidad, es decir, emplear un sistema de regeneración natural de tal modo que sus características esenciales se mantengan intactas y sus especies se reproduzca de manera natural. Obviamente, los proyectos integran cisternas de recolección de aguas pluviales o aljibes de reserva para grandes precipitaciones concebidos y realzados de modo tan artístico que el observador necesitará fijarse un par de veces para percatarse de lo que allí se esconde. O tal vez incluso semejante concepción no se haga visible hasta que se explique expresamente, lo que no tiene por qué afectar o sorprender, ya que cada uno de los proyectos presentados en este volumen, cuenta con su propio encanto y produce en sí mismo una reacción en el observador. Se trata de otra facultad artística de los diseñadores de jardines, el saber esconder algo misterioso en cada uno de sus proyectos.

Haike Falkenberg

Introduzione

GARDEN DESIGN oggi, ossia giardini in tutte le forme e le misure possibili, progettati e realizzati da architetti paesaggistici, ideatori di giardini, architetti o artisti. Per il successo di uno di tali progetti non è determinante la grandezza del terreno, la sua posizione o l'ambiente circostante, se è privato, aziendale o di pubblico utilizzo, né tanto meno lo è il budget prefissato per l'esecuzione e la manutenzione. Molto più importante è che il designer del giardino lavori a stretto contatto con l'architetto dell'edificio e con il proprietario del terreno, in modo che l'organizzazione degli spazi vitali interni ed esterni proceda di pari passo assecondando i desideri e le forme di utilizzo.

Partendo da questo presupposto, vengono realizzati tra l'altro stabili adibiti ad uffici, in cui l'atmosfera lavorativa è migliorata in modo talmente significativo, grazie agli spazi verdi perfettamente organizzati, che il numero di assenze per malattia è stato sensibilmente ridotto. Inoltre, vengono notevolmente abbassati i costi per l'energia. Oggigiorno si trovano dei giardini dove forse a volte non ce lo si aspetterebbe, per esempio sui tetti, dove con il loro verde rendono accessibili nuovi spazi vitali e rappresentano un evidente miglioramento della qualità delle abitazioni e della vita. Al contempo eliminano almeno in parte l'effetto negativo della sigillatura delle superfici e tengono conto di un importante aspetto: il rapporto rispettoso con la natura, e, nel migliore dei casi, viene preso in considerazione anche il concetto di sostenibilità. Ciò significa che viene utilizzato un sistema naturale rigenerabile in modo che rimanga intatto nelle sue caratteristiche essenziali e capace di far ricrescere per le precipitazioni abbondanti vengono integrati nel progetto in modo naturale e acquistano un significato artistico, così che l'osservatore dovrà probabilmente guardarli due o tre volte per capire cosa c'è dietro. È possibile che una tale concezione gli si riveli solo dopo spiegazioni esplicite, e questo non meraviglia e tanto meno disturba, perché ognuno dei progetti qui presentati esercita un fascino particolare e un suo effetto sull'osservatore. Questo dipende da un ulteriore artificio adoperato con maestria dagli esperti di design del giardino, e cioè quello di nascondere in ogni progetto anche qualcosa di misterioso.

Haike Falkenberg

Jardin des Hesperides

Québec I Canada

Landscape design: Cao | Perrot Studio
Los Angeles, California, USA + Paris, France
www.caoperrotstudio.com
Photos: Cao | Perrot Studio, Louise Tanguay, Yvan Maltais

Lined with iris and vetiver, the paths of this garden on the shore of the St Lawrence first lead to an orange grove seemingly floating on the surface of a pond and then into a "lantern" that's fragrant with the essential oils from the plants used here.

Die von Iris und Vetiver gesäumten Wege dieses Gartens am Ufer des Sankt Lorenz führen zunächst zu einem Orangenhain, der auf dem Wasserspiegel eines Teiches zu schweben scheint, und schließlich in eine „Laterne", in der essentielle Öle der hier verwendeten Pflanzen duften.

Les sentiers de ce jardin sur la rive du Saint-Laurent sont bordés d'iris et de vétiver. Ils mènent à une orangeraie qui semble flotter sur un miroir d'eau, puis à une « lanterne ». Elle exhale un parfum composé des huiles extraites des plantes présentes dans le jardin.

Las veredas repletas de lirios y vetiveres de este jardín a orillas del San Lorenzo conducen a un naranjal que parece flotar sobre la superficie de una laguna, y finalizan en un "farol", en el que despiden sus aromas los aceites esenciales extraídos de las especies vegetales plantadas.

Le stradine fiancheggiate da iris e vetiveria di questo giardino sulle sponde del San Lorenzo portano prima di tutto a un aranceto, che sembra come sospeso sullo specchio d'acqua di un lago, e poi ad una "lanterna", nella quale emanano il loro profumo gli oli estratti dalle piante qui utilizzate.

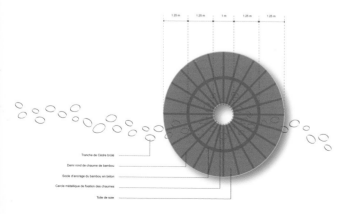

Tranche de Cèdre brûlé
Demi rond de chaume de bambou
Socle d'ancrage du bambou en béton
Cercle métallique de fixation des chaumes
Toile de soie

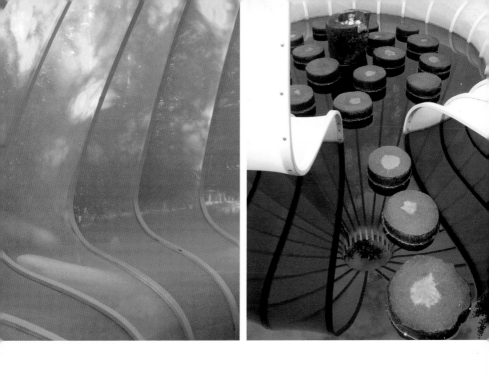

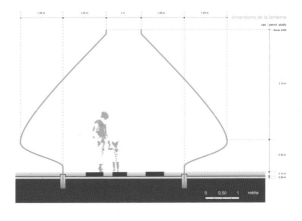

Arthur Ross Terrace

New York City I New York, USA

Rose and Priest Center for Earth and Space at the American Museum of Natural History

Landscape architecture: Charles Anderson Landscape Architecture with Kathryn Gustafson and
Polshek Partnership Architects (architectural project)
Seattle, Washington, USA
www.charlesanderson.com
Photos: N. Beattie-Vallespir, D. Finnin/AMNH, DBOX

In front of the planetarium at the natural history museum, granite in graduated shades and sloping
areas of lawn cast the shadows of a moon, which can be staged in various ways for special events by
means of interactive fountains and light fixtures arranged in the shape of the Orion constellation.

Vor dem Planetarium des Naturkundemuseums zeichnen Granit in unterschiedlichen Schattierungen
und geneigte Grasflächen den Schatten eines Mondes, der durch interaktive Wasserspiele und in der
Orion-Formation arrangierte Lampen zu besonderen Anlässen unterschiedlich in Szene gesetzt
werden kann.

En face du planétarium du musée d'histoire naturelle, du granit dans des dégradés de couleurs et des
pans de pelouse en pente forment les contours d'une lune. Cette lune peut être mise en scène de
différentes manières pour des événements particuliers grâce à des jeux d'eau interactives et à des
lampes disposées selon la constellation d'Orion.

Delante del planetario del Museo de Ciencias Naturales, el granito en diversas tonalidades y las
superficies de césped en pendiente conforman la silueta de una luna, que mediante fuentes interactivas
y con focos dispuestas en formación de Orión, se puede configurar de formas diferentes según la ocasión.

Davanti al planetario del museo di scienze naturali il granito in diverse sfumature e le zone erbose
inclinate disegnano l'ombra della luna che, grazie ai giochi d'acqua interattivi e alle luci disposte secondo la costellazione dell'Orione, può essere allestita in modi diversi per particolari occasioni.

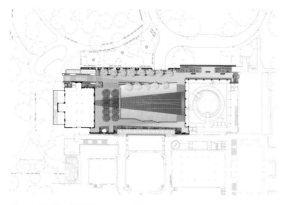

Akili Museum of Art

Jakarta I Indonesia

Landscape architecture: Grain & Green
Tangerang, Indonesia + Singapore, Singapore
www.grainandgreen.com
Photos: courtesy Grain & Green

In Indonesia, the term *alun alun* means a yard for gatherings, dances and ceremonies. In this museum ensemble with its typically Indonesian wall enclosure, the grassy *alun alun* complements the Zen-like garden landscape and perpetuates the tranquil aura of the structures.

Unter *Alun Alun* versteht man in Indonesien einen Hof für Zusammenkünfte, Tänze und Zeremonien. In diesem Museumsensemble mit seiner landestypischen Mauereinfassung ergänzt der grasbewachsene *Alun Alun* die zen-artige Gartenlandschaft und führt die ruhige Ausstrahlung der Gebäude fort.

En Indonésie, le mot *alun alun* désigne une cour où ont lieu rassemblements, danses et cérémonies. Dans ce musée avec son mur d'enceinte typique du pays, l'*alun alun* planté d'herbe vient parachever l'aménagement paysager zen et prolonger l'aura de sérénité des bâtiments.

Alun Alun significa en indonesio espacio en el que celebrar reuniones, bailes o ceremonias. En este complejo de museos, amurallado al estilo autóctono, el *Alun Alun* cubierto de grama sirve de complemento al paisaje ajardinado *zen* y transmite la misma sensación de paz que emana del edificio.

In Indonesia l'espressione *Alun Alun* indica un cortile per i raduni, le danze e le cerimonie. In questo complesso in cui si trova il museo, circondato da una cinta muraria tipica del posto, l'*Alun Alun* con la sua erba verde completa il paesaggio zen del giardino, continuando ad infondere la stessa tranquillità dell'edificio.

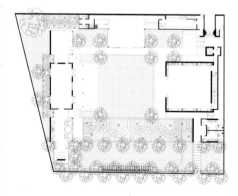

Treasury Courtyards

London I UK

Landscape architecture: Gustafson Porter Ltd
London, UK
www.gustafson-porter.com
Photos: courtesy Foster and Partners

The central axis running through the building and two inner courtyards spans the pool of one of the courtyards as a causeway. Whilst in the second courtyard the causeway passes between verdant green hedges, ringed by a water rill.

Die zentrale Achse, die das Gebäude und zwei Innenhöfe durchläuft, überquert als erhöhter Weg das Wasserbecken des einen Innenhofes. Während im zweiten Innenhof der Weg durch grüne Hecken, umgeben von schmalen Wasserläufen führt.

L'axe central qui parcourt le bâtiment et deux cours intérieures traverse le bassin d'une des cours sous la forme d'une allée surélevée. Tandis que dans la seconde cour, l'allée passe entre des haies verdoyantes, entourée par un petit ruisseau.

El eje central, que atraviesa el edificio y dos patios interiores, cruza en forma de paso elevado el estanque de uno de los patios. Mientras en el segundo patio el pavimento pasa entre los verdes setos, circundado por el canal de agua.

Una strada rialzata attraversa la vasca situata in uno dei cortili lungo l'asse centrale che passa per l'edificio e i cortili interni. Mentre nel secondo cortile il lastricato passa attraverso le siepi verdi aspre, circondate da un ruscello d'acqua.

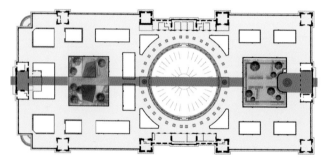

Akademieplatz

Berlin I Germany

Architecture: Levin Monsigny Landschaftsarchitekten
Berlin, Germany
www.levin-monsigny.com
Photos: Claas Dreppenstedt

The square forms the prestigious entrance of the building ensemble in the new science district of Berlin. Freestanding Mountain Ash trees define the open lawn, setting accents during the various seasons. The "decorative windows" with their low plants and metallic symbols bring out the spirit of research.

Im neuen Wissenschaftsviertel Berlins bildet der Platz den repräsentativen Eingang des Gebäudeensembles. Freistehene Ebereschen strukturieren die offene Rasenfläche und setzen Akzente in den verschiedenen Jahreszeiten. Die „Zierfenster" mit niedrigen Pflanzen und metallenen Zeichen wecken den Forschergeist.

La place forme l'entrée prestigieuse d'un ensemble de bâtiments, situé dans le nouveau quartier des sciences de Berlin. Des sorbiers isolés structurent les pelouses ouvertes et donnent le ton, au fil des saisons. Les « fenêtres décoratives » avec leurs plantes basses et leurs symboles métalliques éveillent l'esprit de recherche.

En la nueva zona científica de Berlín, esta plaza simboliza la entrada al conjunto de edificios. Serbales aislados estructuran la superficie de césped y le dan un toque especial en cada una de las cuatro estaciones. Los "ventanales decorativos" con plantas pequeñas y símbolos metálicos apelan al espíritu investigador.

Nel nuovo quartiere scientifico di Berlino la piazza costituisce l'ingresso di rappresentanza del complesso degli edifici. I sorbi selvatici piantati qua e là danno forma alla superficie erbosa aperta e assumono colori diversi a seconda delle stagioni. Le "finestre ornamentali" con le piante basse e le targhette metalliche risvegliano lo spirito di ricerca.

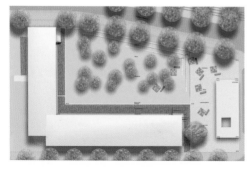

Bertelsmann Unter den Linden 1

Berlin I Germany

Architecture: Levin Monsigny Landschaftsarchitekten
Berlin, Germany
www.levin-monsigny.com
Photos: Claas Dreppenstedt

The soft form of the two semi-circles adds new life to the wide sidewalk of stately Unter den Linden boulevard while simultaneously highlighting the building like a gesture of generosity. Variegated species of box tree hedges are enclosed by low borders (architectural bronze on high-grade steel).

Die weiche Form der beiden Halbkreise verjüngt den breiten Gehweg des Prachtboulevards Unter den Linden und leitet gleichzeitig mit großzügiger Geste zum Gebäude. Die Buchsbaumhecken unterschiedlich farbiger Sorten werden von niedrigen Einfassungen (Baubronze auf Edelstahl) eingerahmt.

La forme douce des deux demi-cercles rajeunit le large trottoir du grand boulevard Unter den Linden et dirige également les visiteurs vers l'immeuble dans un geste généreux. Les haies de buis de différentes espèces sont bordées de clôtures basses en acier inoxydable recouvert de bronze.

Las suaves formas de estos dos semicírculos sirven para remozar las amplias aceras del opulento bulevar Unter den Linden, al tiempo que conducen al edificio o con un toque de grandeza. Los setos de boj de diferentes clases y colores sestán rodeados por unas estructuras bajas a modo de cerco con bronces arquitectónicos sobre acero inoxidable.

La forma morbida dei due semicerchi dà nuova vita all'ampia strada pedonale dello splendido boulevard Unter den Linden, descrivendo nel contempo un ampio movimento che guida verso l'edificio. Le aiuole di bosso composte da varietà di diversi colori sono incorniciate da recinzioni basse (bronzo da costruzione su acciaio inossidabile).

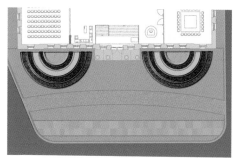

Carlebach Park

Lübeck I Germany

Architecture: Levin Monsigny Landschaftsarchitekten
Berlin, Germany
www.levin-monsigny.com
Photos: Claas Dreppenstedt

Trees serve as the central creators of space and unite the classic notions of open space into a whole: the urban esplanade to the north with the promenade as its counterpart, the spacious lawn and the lawn terraces with their many different opportunities for play and sports.

Bäume dienen als zentrale Raumbildner und fügen die klassischen Freiraumtypen zu einem Ganzen zusammen: die städtische Esplanade im Norden mit dem Gegenüber der Promenade, dazwischen die weitläufige Rasenfläche und die mit vielseitigen Spiel- und Sportangeboten ausgestatteten Rasenterrassen.

Les arbres servent à articuler l'espace et à réunir en un tout les différents espaces ouverts classiques : l'esplanade urbaine au nord avec la promenade en contrepoint, la vaste pelouse et les terrasses en herbe équipées pour divers sports et loisirs.

Aquí los árboles son los principales configuradores del espacio, aunando en un todo los modelos clásicos de ordenación del espacio de ocio: una explanada urbana al norte; enfrente, un paseo; entre ambos, una amplia extensión de césped junto a otras aterrazadas también con césped y dotadas con áreas de juego y equipamientos deportivos multiusos.

Gli alberi rivestono la funzione principale di organizzazione dello spazio riunendo i tipi classici di spazio aperto in un tutt'uno: l'Esplanade della città a nord di fronte la passeggiata a nord, la spaziosa superficie erbosa e le terrazze ricoperte d'erba con aree da gioco e aree sportive multiuso.

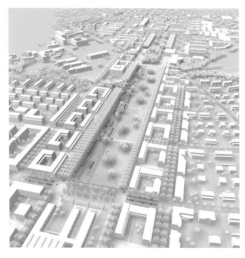

Japanese Garden Berlin

Berlin I Germany

Landscape architecture: Shunmyo Masuno
Yokohama, Japan
www.kenkohji.jp/s
Photos: Minao Tabata

The water that starts out by gushing down a waterfall in the southeastern part of this garden symbolizes the origin and historical development of Germany. A reflecting pond surrounded by lawn stands for the country's modern history, while the pavilion represents the people living in the present age.

Der Wasserlauf, der im Südosten des Gartens über einen Wasserfall sprudelt, symbolisiert den Ursprung und die geschichtliche Entwicklung Deutschlands. Ein spiegelnder See im mit Rasen gestalteten Bereich steht für die moderne Geschichte und der Pavillon repräsentiert das Volk, das in der Gegenwart lebt.

L'eau qui jaillit d'une chute d'eau au sud-est du jardin symbolise l'origine et le développement historique de l'Allemagne. Un étang aux multiples reflets dans l'espace avec pelouse représente l'histoire moderne, alors que le pavillon symbolise les personnes vivant dans l'ère contemporaine.

La corriente de agua, que termina batiéndose en una cascada en la cara sudeste del jardín, simboliza los orígenes y la evolución histórica de Alemania. El estanque de aguas reverberantes en un área de césped refleja la historia moderna; mientras, el pabellón representa al pueblo que vive en el presente.

L'acqua che zampilla dalla cascata nella parte sud-orientale del giardino simboleggia l'origine e lo sviluppo storico della Germania. Un lago limpido posto in un'area adibita a prato rappresenta la storia moderna, mentre il padiglione raffigura il popolo che vive nel presente.

Rensho.ji

Yokohama I Japan

Landscape architecture: Shunmyo Masuno
Yokohama, Japan
www.kenkohji.jp/s
Photos: Minao Tabata

This temple structure was actually founded in the 14ᵗʰ century by a monk named Rensho. The many stones of the garden, which merge into a "river" of stones leading to the newly constructed entrance hall, symbolize a deluge of drops merging to form a deep stream.

Diese Tempelanlage wurde bereits im 14. Jahrhundert von einem Mönch namens Rensho gegründet. Die vielen Steine des Gartens, die in einen auf die neu errichtete Eingangshalle ausgerichteten „Fluss" aus Steinen münden, symbolisieren eine Vielzahl von Tropfen, die zusammen einen tiefen Strom bilden.

La structure de ce temple a été fondée dès le XIVème siècle par un moine nommé Rensho. Les nombreuses pierres du jardin, qui mènent à une « rivière » de pierres en direction du hall d'entrée récemment construit, symbolisent une myriade de gouttes d'eau qui forment une profonde rivière.

Este jardín, enmarcado en un templo, fue concebido en el siglo XIV por un monje llamado Rensho. Las incontables piedras, que desembocan en un "río" pétreo dirigido hacia el nuevo vestíbulo, simbolizan la diversidad de las gotas que, en su conjunto, conforman una corriente profunda.

Questo tempio fu fondato già nel XIV secolo da un monaco di nome Rensho. Le numerose pietre del giardino, che confluiscono in un "fiume" di pietre orientato verso la nuova sala d'ingresso, simboleggiano una molteplicità di gocce che insieme formano un profondo torrente.

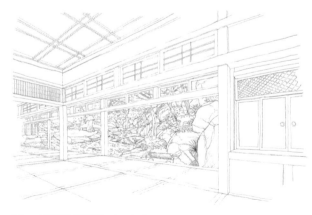

Bavarian National Museum

Munich I Germany

Landscape architecture: Rainer Schmidt Landscape Architects
Munich + Berlin + Bernburg, Germany
www.rainerschmidt.com
Photos: Sirtoli Schnell, Vehes

The square in front of the museum has been reinterpreted on the basis of a sunken parterre of flowers, which influenced many square designs at the beginning of the last century. Granite strips cover the area like a carpet, while pruned *Buxus sempervierens* and magnolias add structure in groups of four.

Der Museumsvorplatz wurde auf der Basis eines vertieften Blumenparterre, das viele Platzgestaltungen Anfang des vergangenen Jahrhunderts beeinflusst hat, neuinterpretiert. Wie ein Teppich überziehen Granitstreifen die Fläche, während geschnittene *Buxus sempervierens* und Magnolien in Vierergruppen für Struktur sorgen.

Le parvis du musée a été réinterprété à partir d'un parterre de fleurs encaissé, comme en comptaient de nombreuses places au début du siècle dernier. Des bandes de granit couvrent l'espace comme un tapis, tandis que des massifs taillés de buis toujours vert (*Buxus sempervirens*) et des magnolias en groupes de quatre structurent l'ensemble.

La anteplaza del museo se ha reinterpretado basándose en un parterre floral que al principio del siglo pasado tuvo mucho que decir en la configuración de la plaza. Las hileras de granito cubren la superficie a modo de alfombras, junto a *Buxus sempervierens* podados y magnolias en grupos de cuatro, que confieren estructura a la composición.

La piazza antistante il museo è stata reinterpretata a partire dal parterre di fiori ad incasso, che ha influenzato molti progetti di piazze dell'inizio del secolo scorso. Le strisce di granito ricoprono la superficie come un tappeto, mentre i *Buxus sempervierens* spuntati e le magnolie disposte in gruppi di quattro ne sottolineano la struttura.

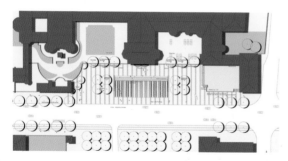

Sunken Gardens of Riempark

Munich I Germany

Landscape architecture: Rainer Schmidt Landscape Architects
Munich + Berlin + Bernburg, Germany
www.rainerschmidt.com
Photos: Rainer Schmidt, dpa, J. Rosskamp, Stefan Müller-Naumann

One portion of this landscape park was designed for the BUGA Munich Garden Exhibition 2005 and is now open to the public. The designers never swayed from their leitmotif—sustainability. The graphic patterns of the park are derived from the basic structural patterns of organic matter, such as extremely minimized or maximized versions of leaf cells.

Ein Teil dieses Landschaftsparks wurde für die BUGA München 2005 gestaltet und ist heute öffentlich, dabei fand der Leitgedanke der Nachhaltigkeit konsequent Anwendung. Die grafischen Muster basieren auf strukturellen Grundmustern des Organischen, z.B. Blattzellen, in extremer Verkleinerung bzw. Vergrößerung.

Une partie de ce jardin paysager, conçue en 2005 pour le BUGA de Munich (Exposition horticole allemande), est désormais ouverte au public. Ici, le principe du développement durable a été appliqué de façon systématique. Les motifs graphiques sont inspirés de motifs structurels organiques, comme par exemple des cellules de feuilles microscopiques ou agrandies au maximum.

Una parte de este jardín paisajístico, actualmente público, fue concebida en el año 2005 para el BUGA muniqués, aplicando la tesis de la sostenibilidad de forma consecuente. Las formas se basan en los modelos orgánicos, como por ejemplo los de las células vegetales, minimizados o ampliados al exremo.

Una parte di questo parco paesaggistico è stato allestito nel 2005 per la mostra di giardinaggio BUGA di Monaco ed è oggi aperto al pubblico. Qui ha trovato coerente applicazione il concetto ispiratore della sostenibilità. I disegni grafici si fondano sui disegni strutturali di base del mondo organico, per es. Le cellule della foglia, estremamente rimpiccioliti o ingranditi.

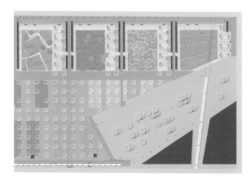

PUBLIC SPACES . Sunken Gardens of Riempark

Loki Areal

Winterthur I Switzerland

Landscape architecture: Rotzler Krebs Partner Landschaftsarchitekten
Winterthur, Switzerland
www.rkp.ch
Photos: courtesy Rotzler Krebs Partner Landschaftsarchitekten

The fences and gates of this former railroad complex with a locomotive factory have been removed. New walkways now link this area to its district. Formally painted-over markings along with red-painted guardrails, benches and trunks define the colors of the space and illuminate change and new beginnings.

Zäune und Tore des ehemaligen Eisenbahngeländes mit Lokomotivfabrik wurden entfernt. Neue Fußwege binden das Areal nun in das Stadtviertel ein. Formal überzeichnete Markierungen sowie rot lackierte Leitplanken, Sitzbänke und Stämme prägen den Raum farblich und machen auf Wandel und Aufbruch aufmerksam.

Les barrières et les portes de cet ancien complexe ferroviaire comportant une usine de locomotives ont été enlevées. De nouveaux trottoirs relient à présent cette zone au quartier de la ville. Des inscriptions marquages suraccentués, ainsi que des rambardes, des bancs et des troncs peints en rouge mettent de la couleur dans cet espace et attirent l'attention sur les mutations et les nouveaux départs.

Se eliminaron las verjas y los portalones de un antiguo recinto de ferrocarriles. Los nuevos senderos comunican este espacio con el barrio contiguo. Las señalizaciones dominantes junto al vallado, los bancos y los troncos en rojo dan un toque de color al espacio y resaltan la transformación experimentada.

I recinti e i portoni dell'ex zona ferroviaria con la fabbrica di locomotive sono stati rimossi. Questa zona è ora collegata al resto del quartiere attraverso nuove strade pedonali. Segnaletica orizzontale più marcata, insieme a guardrail, panchine e tronchi verniciati di rosso, danno colore all'ambiente focalizzando l'attenzione sul mutamento e sulla voglia di partire.

Charlotte Garden

Copenhagen I Denmark

Architecture: SLA
Copenhagen, Denmark
www.sla.dk
Photos: SLA, Torben Petersen

Various species of grass such as *Festuca glauca*, *Seslevia* and *Molina caerulea* with their hues changing from blue and green to winter gold produce magical colors year-round in this multi-purpose garden. The interplay of intertwining forms and colors is very inviting.

Verschiedene Grassorten wie *Festuca glauca*, *Seslevia* und *Molina caerulea* mit ihren von blau über grün zu winterlichem Gold changierenden Tönen zaubern das ganze Jahr über Farbe in diesen vielfältig genutzten Garten. Das Zusammenspiel der ineinander greifenden Formen und Farben wirkt sehr einladend.

Dans ce jardin aux multiples fonctions, de nombreuses variétés d'herbes comme la *Festuca glauca*, la *Seslevia* et la *Molina caerulea*, aux teintes passant du bleu et du vert aux tons dorés de l'hiver, enchantent le visiteur tout au long de l'année. L'interaction entre les formes et les couleurs entremê-lées est très attrayante.

Diferentes herbáceas como la *Festuca glauca*, la *Seslevia* y la *Molina caerulea*, con cambiantes tonos desde azules y verdes hasta los dorados de invierno, crean fascinantes juegos de color durante todo el año en este jardín multiusos. Sus movimientos de colores y formas engarzadas resultan especialmente atrayentes.

Le diverse varietà di erba come la *Festuca glauca*, la *Seslevia* e la *Molina caerulea*, con le loro tonalità che cambiano dal blu al verde fino all'oro in inverno, portano la magia del colore in questo giardino multiuso per tutto l'arco dell'anno. L'interazione delle forme e dei colori che si integrano tra loro è molto invitante.

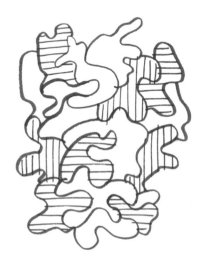

University of San Francisco
School of Business & Administration

San Francisco I California, USA

Architecture: T. Delaney – Seam Studios
San Francisco, California, USA
www.tdelaney.com
Photos: Topher Delaney

Students of the business school here can look at the green-blue world map showing the most vital trade routes either by sitting on alternately black or white concrete benches reflecting the central design theme of a barcode or by sitting on black concrete orbs.

Die Studenten der Wirtschaftsuniversität können zum Betrachten der grün-blauen Weltkarte mit den wichtigsten Handelsrouten auf den abwechselnd schwarzen oder weißen Betonbänken, die das zentrale Entwurfsthema des Barcodes aufnehmen, oder auch auf den schwarzen Betonkugeln Platz nehmen.

Les étudiants de la faculté de commerce ont le choix pour s'asseoir quand ils observent la carte bleu-vert du monde indiquant les principales routes commerciales : sur les bancs de béton alternativement noirs et blancs qui évoquent le code-barre, thème central du design, ou sur les boules de béton noir.

Para admirar el mapamundi verdiazul con las rutas comerciales más importantes, los estudiantes de la facultad de Economía pueden tomar asiento en los bancos de hormigón que alternan entre el blanco y el negro, siguiendo el tema central del código de barras, o también en una de las esferas negras de concreto.

Per osservare il planisfero blu e verde con le più importanti rotte commerciali, gli studenti della facoltà di economia possono accomodarsi sulle panchine di cemento alternate in bianco e nero, che riprendono il tema centrale di progettazione del codice a barre, oppure sulle sfere nere di cemento.

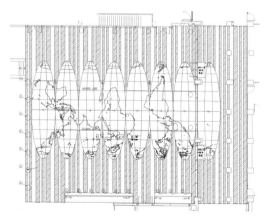

Kindergarden Griechische Allee

Berlin I Germany

Architecture: BEHLES & JOCHIMSEN ARCHITECTURE
Landscape architecture: TOPOTEK 1
Berlin, Germany
www.topotek1.de
Photos: Hanns Joosten

The ramp sculpture starting on the upper floor surrounds the property, separates it from the street and is important for wheelchair access. The playground equipment was integrated based on customer specifications to maximize open space and to preserve longstanding trees on the property.

Die am Obergeschoss des Gebäudes ansetzende Rampenskulptur umfasst das Grundstück, grenzt es zur Straße ab und ist wichtig für den behindertengerechten Zugang. Spielgeräte sind maßgeschneidert integriert, sodass die Freiflächen maximiert und alter Baumbestand erhalten werden konnte.

La rampe sculpée à partir de l'étage supérieur entoure la propriété, la sépare de la rue et joue un rôle important pour l'accès en fauteuil roulant. Les installations de jeux ont été spécialement adaptées au terrain pour optimiser les espaces ouverts et préserver les vieux arbres.

La escultura a base de rampas de la planta superior de este edificio ocupa todo el terreno, lo separa de la calle y juega un papel primordial en el acceso adaptado a discapacitados. Los columpios se integran perfectamente en las rampas con el fin de maximizar el espacio libre y conservar los árboles originales.

La scultura a rampe unita al piano superiore dell'edificio circonda il terreno, lo separa dalla strada e garantisce l'accesso ai disabili. I giochi sono stati inseriti su misura, in modo da avere quanti più è possibile spazi aperti e conservare i vecchi alberi.

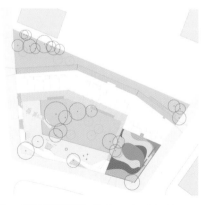

Genzyme Center

Cambridge I Massachusetts, USA

Architecture and general planners: Behnisch Architects, Inc.
Venice, California, USA
Gardens with LOG ID, Tübingen, Germany
www.behnisch.com
Photos: Anton Grassl, Stefan Behnisch

Ingenious planning of daylight ensures the growth of many plants in this administrative center designed around an atrium. At the same time, it enhances both the spatial quality and economic efficiency of this award-winning pioneer building of "green" design strategies for business architecture.

Ausgeklügelte Tageslichtplanung ermöglicht das Wachstum vieler Pflanzen in dieser rund um ein Atrium konzipierten Hauptverwaltung. Gleichzeitig wird die Raumqualität sowie die Wirtschaftlichkeit dieses preisgekrönten Pioniergebäudes „grüner" Planungsstrategien für Unternehmensarchitektur verbessert.

Une planification ingénieuse de la lumière naturelle permet la croissance de nombreuses plantes dans ce siège social conçu autour d'un atrium. Parallèlement ont été améliorées la qualité spatiale et l'efficacité économique de ce bâtiment, primé, et pionnier en matière de stratégies « vertes » pour l'architecture d'entreprise.

La elaborada planificación de la luz diurna posibilita el crecimiento de muchas plantas en este edificio central de administratión concebido en torno a un atrio. Al mismo tiempo, se mejora la productividad y calidad del espacio del galardonado edificio, pionero en estrategias "verdes" de arquitectura empresarial.

Una sofisticata pianificazione della luce del giorno rende possibile la crescita di molte piante in questa sede centrale, concepita tutta intorno a un atrio. Al contempo viene migliorata la qualità dello spazio e l'economicità di questo premiato edificio, precursore delle strategie urbanistiche "verdi" per l'architettura aziendale.

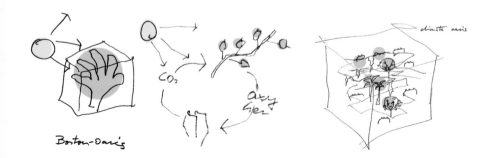

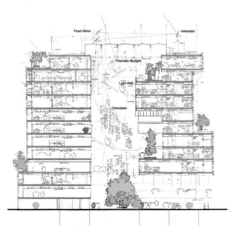

TDCCBR
Terrence Donnelly Centre for Cellular and Biomolecular Research

Toronto I Canada

Architecture: Behnisch Architekten, Stuttgart, Germany
with architectsAlliance, Toronto, Canada
Landscape with Diana Gerrard Landscape Architecture, Toronto, Canada
www.behnisch.com
Photos: David Cook, Stefan Behnisch

Two and three-story green spaces in the upper floors of this research center are places for informal encounters or breaks. The selection of plants gives each garden its own character. The foliage provides shade in the summer, while allowing closer views of the inside during the winter.

Zwei- und dreigeschossige Grünräume in den Obergeschossen des Forschungszentrums sind Orte für informelle Begegnungen oder Pausen. Jeder Garten hat durch die Auswahl der Pflanzen seinen eigenen Charakter. Das Laub spendet Schatten im Sommer, während die Blicke im Winter tiefer in das Gebäude gelangen.

Les espaces verts sur deux et trois niveaux dans les étages supérieurs de ce centre de recherche sont propices aux rencontres informelles ou aux pauses. Chaque jardin a son propre caractère selon les plantes choisies. Les feuilles donnent de l'ombre en été, tandis qu'en hiver la vue sur l'intérieur du bâtiment est plus dégagée.

Los espacios verdes de dos y tres plantas ubicados en las plantas superiores de este centro de investigación son lugares para encuentros informales o descansos. Cada jardín tiene un propio carácter determinado por la selección de plantas. El follaje regala sombra en verano, y en invierno pone a la vista el edificio.

Gli spazi verdi su due e tre livelli nei piani superiori del centro di ricerca sono i luoghi per gli incontri informali o per le pause. La scelta di piante diverse conferisce ad ogni giardino un proprio carattere. Le foglie danno ombra in estate, mentre gli sguardi penetrano più profondamente nell'edificio d'inverno.

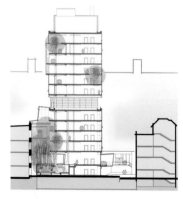

A Four Season Parterre

Milan I Italy

Landscape architecture: Patrizia Pozzi with Gianmaria e Roberto Beretta (architectural project), Hydroware (green realizations)
Milan, Italy
www.patriziapozzi.it
Photos: Patrizia Pozzi

Erica vulgaris in fall, *Viola cornuta* in winter, *Primula vulgaris* in spring, and *Impatiens "New Guinea"* in the summer give the parterre de broderie its multitude of colors. Its lines present a playfully enhanced Baroque design that elegantly conceals the roof of a parking garage at this corporate headquarters.

Erica vulgaris im Herbst, *Viola cornuta* im Winter, *Primula vulgaris* im Frühling und *Impatiens „New Guinea"* im Sommer färben das Broderieparterre bunt. Seine Linien sind ein auf spielerische Weise vergrößerter barocker Entwurf und verhüllen elegant das Tiefgaragendach dieses Firmensitzes.

Erica vulgaris en automne, *Viola cornuta* en hiver, *Primula vulgaris* au printemps et *Impatiens « New Guinea »* en été donnent des couleurs vives à ce parterre de broderie. Ses lignes suivent un dessin baroque qui a été agrandi de manière ludique et qui cache élégamment le toit du parking du siège de la société.

La *Erica vulgaris* en otoño, la *Viola cornuta* en invierno, la *Primula vulgaris* en primavera y la *Impatiens "New Guinea"* en verano dan color a este parterre de filigrana. Sus graciosas líneas a modo de boceto barroco aumentado, cubren con elegancia el tejado del garaje subterráneo de la central de esta compañía.

L'*Erica vulgaris* in autunno, la *Viola cornuta* in inverno, la *Primula vulgaris* in primavera e l'*Impatiens "New Guinea"* in estate rendono variopinti i ricami del parterre de broderie. Le sue linee sono un disegno barocco ingrandito in modo giocoso e nascondono elegantemente il tetto del garage sotterraneo di questa sede aziendale.

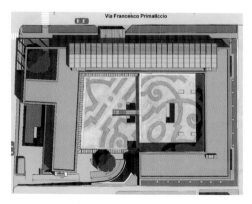

The succession of parterre in the four seasons:
Primula vulgaris for spring

The succession of parterre in the four seasons:
Viola cornuta for winter

Casa Nueva Office

Santa Barbara I California, USA

Architecture: Blackbird Architects
Landscape architecture: Van Atta Associates
Santa Barbara, California, USA
www.va-la.com
Photos: Saxon Holt, Bill Dewey

Flowering wisteria and fabric along the 360-feet long trellis protect the south and west side of this building from excessive heat. A rock designed by an artist covers a cistern for rainwater, which is collected and filtered in an ornamental bioswale that extends through the courtyard and the plants there.

Blühende Glyzinien und Stoff entlang der 110 Meter langen Rankgitter schützen die Süd- und Westseite des Gebäudes vor Überhitzung. Der von einem Künstler gestaltete Stein bedeckt eine Zisterne für Regenwasser, das in einer ornamentalen Senke, die den bepflanzten Hof durchzieht, gesammelt und gefiltert wird.

Des glycines en fleurs et des tissus le long du treillis de 110 mètres de long protègent le sud et l'ouest du bâtiment de la chaleur. Une pierre conçue par un artiste couvre une citerne d'eau de pluie, qui est collectée et filtrée dans une baissière ornementale qui traverse les plantations de la cour.

Las glicinias en flor y diversas telas a lo largo de los 110 metros de enrejado protegen contra el calor las caras sur y oeste del edificio. Una losa diseñada por un artista cubre un aljibe para aguas pluviales, recogidas y filtradas en un cauce ornamental que recorre el patio cubierto de plantas.

Il glicine in fiore e la stoffa posti lungo i 110 metri del graticcio proteggono dal surriscaldamento il lato sud e quello ovest dell'edificio. Una lastra in pietra eseguita da un artista ricopre una cisterna per l'acqua piovana, raccolta e filtrata in una canaletta ornamentale che attraversa il cortile con le piante.

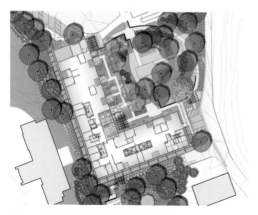

Lufthansa Aviation Center

Frankfurt am Main I Germany

Architecture: Ingenhoven Architects
Düsseldorf, Germany
Landscape architecture: WKM Landschaftsarchitekten Weber Klein Maas
Meerbusch, Germany – www.wkm-la.de
Photos: H.G. Esch, Hennef

The double ridge structure of this building frames every office wing with two landscaped atriums serving as buffers against noise and air pollution. They also save energy and can be used by employees and visitors alike. The design themes from the five continents symbolize the international links of the company.

Die Doppel-Kammstruktur des Gebäudes rahmt jeden Büroflügel mit zwei begrünten Atrien ein, die Lärm- und Klimapuffer sind, Energie sparen und sowohl von Mitarbeitern als auch von Besuchern genutzt werden können. Die Gestaltungsthemen aus den fünf Kontinenten symbolisieren die weltweiten Verbindungen des Unternehmens.

La structure à double faîtage du bâtiment encadre chaque aile de bureaux avec deux atriums verts qui servent de barrage à la pollution atmosphérique et sonore. Ils économisent de l'énergie et peuvent être utilisés par les employés tout comme par les visiteurs. Les thématiques de design empruntées aux cinq continents symbolisent les relations internationales de l'entreprise.

La estructura en doble peine del edificio encuadra las alas de oficinas mediante dos atrios ajardinados que atenúan el ruido y las temperaturas, ahorran energía y que pueden utilizar tanto empleados como visitantes. La configuración temática basada en los cinco continentes simboliza los nexos globales de la firma.

Grazie alla struttura a doppio pettine dell'edificio ogni ala dell'ufficio è incorniciata da due atri pieni di verde, che proteggono dal rumore e dagli agenti atmosferici, fanno risparmiare energia e possono essere utilizzati sia dai dipendenti che dai visitatori. I temi di allestimento provenienti dai cinque continenti simboleggiano i collegamenti della compagnia con tutto il mondo.

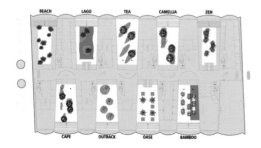

Hillsborough Residence

San Francisco I California, USA

Landscape architecture: Andrea Cochran Landscape Architecture (ACLA)
San Francisco, California, USA
www.acochran.com
Photos: Marion Brenner

In close cooperation with the architect and owner of this villa, ACLA designed all of the villa's outside facilities based on the principal aspects of Feng Shui: space, environment, man and time. In the process, they managed to preserve old oak and redwood trees, which add structure to the harmonic design.

In enger Zusammenarbeit mit Architekt und Eigentümer gestaltete ACLA sämtliche Außenanlagen dieser Villa unter Berücksichtigung der Grundprinzipien des Feng Shui: Raum, Umwelt, Mensch und Zeit. Eine alte Eiche und Redwood-Bäume konnten erhalten werden und geben dem harmonischen Design Struktur.

En coopération étroite avec l'architecte et le propriétaire, ACLA a dessiné toutes les installations extérieures de cette villa, en tenant compte des principes de base du Feng Shui : espace, environnement, occupants et temps. On a également pu préserver un vieux chêne et des séquoias qui structurent le design harmonieux.

ACLA concibió los espacios exteriores de esta residencia, a través de una estrecha colaboración entre arquitecto y propietario y respetando los principios del Feng Shui: espacio, entorno, ser humano y tiempo. Se pudieron conservar una vieja encina y pinos silvestres, que dotan de estructura al armónico diseño.

In stretta collaborazione con l'architetto e il proprietario, ACLA ha allestito gli esterni di questa villa tenendo in considerazione i principi del Feng Shui: spazio, ambiente, uomo e tempo. Si sono potuti conservare una vecchia quercia e le sequoie, che danno forma all'armonico design.

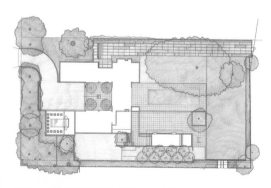

Vego Garden

Pacific Palisades, Santa Monica I California, USA

Landscape design: Cao | Perrot Studio
Los Angeles, California, USA + Paris, France
www.caoperrotstudio.com
Photos: Stephen Jerrom

Located on the hills above the Pacific Coast, this terrace garden has narrow rows of *Stipa tenuifolia* running across it like an optical continuation of the waves breaking in the distance. The moisture of the recurrent fog has a way of stirring up these ornamental grasses and mollifying their strict arrangement.

Auf den Hügeln über der Pazifikküste liegt dieser Terrassengarten, über den sich schmale Reihen *Stipa tenuifolia* wie eine optische Fortsetzung der sich in der Ferne brechenden Wellen ziehen. Die Feuchtigkeit des häufigen Nebels zerzaust diese Ziergräser und lockert so die strenge Gestaltung auf.

Ce jardin sur terrasse est situé sur les collines au-dessus de la côte pacifique. D'étroites rangées de *Stipa tenuifolia* le traversent comme le prolongement optique des vagues se brisant au loin. L'humidité du brouillard fréquent ébouriffe ces cheveux d'ange ornementaux qui apportent de la légèreté dans le strict agencement du jardin.

Desde las colinas donde se ubica este jardín dispuesto en terrazas se divisa la costa del Pacífico. Las delgadas hileras de *Stipa tenuifolia* conforman la continuación visual de las lejanas olas batientes. La humedad proporcionada por la frecuente bruma desenreda la hierba ornamental, aligerando la rígida composición.

Sulle colline prospicienti le coste del Pacifico si trova questo giardino terrazzato, in cui sottili file di *Stipa tenuifolia* proseguono l'effetto ottico delle onde che si infrangono in lontananza. L'umidità della frequente nebbia scompiglia queste erbe ornamentali alleggerendone così la struttura rigida.

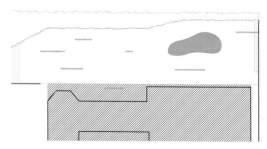

Masia in Emporda

Catalonia I Spain

Architecture: Albert Aguirre, Interior designer: Carles Ferruz
Landscape architecture: Bet Figueras
Barcelona, Spain
www.betfigueras.com
Photos: courtesy Bet Figueras

This structure fuses traditional architecture and modernist, linear elements into an impressive composition. At the same time, the olive trees on the trimmed lawn almost take on the appearance of art objects and the access path resembles an abstractly curved pattern when seen from above.

Das Gebäude verschmelzt traditionelle Architektur mit modernen, gradlinigen Elementen zu einer beeindruckenden Komposition. Analog dazu wirken die Olivenbäume auf dem getrimmten Rasen beinahe wie Kunstobjekte und der Zugangsweg wird von oben gesehen zu einem abstrakt geschwungenen Muster.

Le bâtiment mêle l'architecture traditionnelle avec des éléments modernes, linéaires, dans une composition magistrale. Parallèlement, les oliviers sur la pelouse impeccablement entretenue ont presque l'air d'objets d'art et la voie d'accès, vue d'en haut, évoque un motif abstrait sinueux.

En este edificio se funden la arquitectura tradicional con elementos modernos de líneas rectas. El resultado es una composición impactante. Los olivos se yerguen en el césped recién cortado como obras de arte. Visto desde arriba, el camino forma un abstracto motivo oscilante.

In quest'edificio l'architettura tradizionale si fonde con elementi moderni e rettilinei in una composizione straordinaria. Analogamente gli ulivi sul prato rasato sembrano quasi degli oggetti d'arte e la via d'accesso vista dall'alto diventa un astratto disegno arcuato.

Floating Islands

Shepherd I Montanta, USA

Architecture: Floating Island International
Shepherd, Montana, USA
www.floatingislandinternational.com
Photos: courtesy Floating Island International

BioHavens, the artificial floating islands, open up new avenues in design using water surfaces. They place almost no limits on planting and creative ideas, you can walk on them and they fulfill important filter functions. As a valuable enlargement of shore habitats, they provide living space for many creatures.

BioHavens, die künstlichen Schwimminseln, bieten neue Gestaltungsmöglichkeiten auf Wasserflächen. Sie setzen Bepflanzung und kreativen Ideen fast keine Grenzen, können begehbar sein und erfüllen wichtige Filterfunktionen. Als kostbare Vergrößerung des Uferhabitats sind sie Lebensraum vieler Lebewesen.

Les BioHavens, des îles flottantes artificielles, permettent de nouvelles compositions à la surface de l'eau. Elles offrent des possibilités quasiment infinies de plantation et d'idées créatives, sont accessibles au visiteur et remplissent d'importantes fonctions de filtration. Précieux agrandissement de l'habitat sur le rivage, elles procurent un espace de vie à de nombreuses créatures.

Las BioHavens, o islas flotantes artificiales, ofrecen nuevas posibilidades de configuración en el agua. Las ideas creativas a la hora de plantar no conocen límites, pueden ser transitables y cumplir importantes funciones de filtrado. Al formar una prolongación del hábitat de las riberas, constituyen el espacio natural de muchos seres vivos.

BioHavens, le isole galleggianti artificiali, offrono delle nuove opportunità di allestimento su superfici acquatiche. Quasi non ci sono limiti alle idee creative e alle piante che vi si possono usare, inoltre ci si può salire sopra e adempiono funzioni importanti di filtraggio. Prezioso ampliamento dell'habitat delle rive, sono uno spazio vitale per tanti esseri viventi.

Serene House

Yogyakarta I Indonesia

Landscape architecture: Grain & Green
Tangerang, Indonesia + Singapore, Singapore
www.grainandgreen.com
Photos: courtesy Grain & Green

The garden becomes the heart of this residential building by softening the building's austerity as it radiates peace and cheerfulness. Spacious terraces, shady trees and gentle natural colors help you leave behind the hustle and bustle of your work day in no time. The lighting sets an accent that's magical.

Der Garten wird zum Herzstück der Anlage, indem er die Strenge des Wohnhauses mildert und Ruhe und Heiterkeit ausstrahlt. Großzügige Terrassen, schattenspendende Bäume und sanfte Naturtöne lassen die Hektik des Arbeitstages schnell vergessen. Die Beleuchtung setzt einen magischen Akzent.

En dégageant paix et sérénité, le jardin devient le cœur de la propriété et atténue la sévérité du bâtiment résidentiel. Des terrasses spacieuses, l'ombre des arbres et les couleurs naturelles douces vous feront vite oublier le rythme effréné des journées de travail. L'éclairage donne une touche magique à l'ensemble.

El jardín suaviza las líneas austeras de la vivienda, transmite sosiego y alegría, convirtiéndose así en el centro de la residencia. Amplias terrazas, frondosos árboles con sombra y cálidos tonos naturales permiten olvidar rápidamente el estrés del trabajo. La iluminación aporta un toque mágico.

Il giardino si trasforma nel cuore della struttura, addolcendo la rigidità della casa ed infondendo pace e serenità. Gli ampi terrazzi, insieme agli alberi ombrosi e alle tonalità delicate della natura, fanno rapidamente scordare la frenesia delle giornate lavorative. L'illuminazione conferisce un'atmosfera magica.

PRIVATE SPACES . Serene House   125

Lotus House

East Japan | Japan

Architecture and landscape architecture: Kengo Kuma & Associates
Tokyo, Japan
www.kkaa.co.jp
Photos: Daici Ano

The austerity of this house in the mountains is mollified to some degree by an ingenious steel lattice construction with stone slabs. The grace of this construction is on a par with the garden architecture dominated by tender lotus. This water garden integrates the house into the landscape.

Die Strenge dieses Hauses in den Bergen wird z.T. durch eine ausgeklügelte Stahlgitterkonstruktion mit Steinplatten aufgebrochen. Ihre Leichtigkeit entspricht der Gartenarchitektur, die vor allem von zartem Lotus bestimmt wird. Dieser Wassergarten bindet das Haus in die Landschaft ein.

L'austérité de cette maison dans les montagnes est partiellement atténuée par une structure ingénieuse en treillis d'acier avec des dalles de pierre. Leur légèreté répond à l'architecture du jardin caractérisée principalement par le tendre lotus. Ce jardin d'eau intègre la maison dans le paysage.

La rigidez de esta casa en las montañas se rompe parcialmente mediante un ingenioso enrejado de acero con planchas de piedra. Su ligereza corresponde a la arquitectura del jardín, caracterizada por las delicadas flores de loto. Este jardín acuático enmarca la casa en el conjunto del paisaje.

La rigidità di questa casa di montagna viene in parte spezzata da una sofisticata struttura di barre d'acciaio con lastre di pietra, la cui leggerezza è in armonia con l'architettura del giardino, caratterizzata soprattutto dal delicato fiore di loto. Questo giardino acquatico ingloba la casa nel paesaggio.

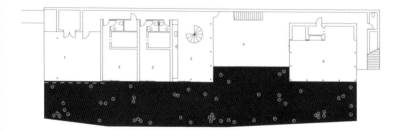

Opus Arisugawa Terrace

Hiroo Shibuya-ku, Tokyo I Japan

Landscape architecture: Shunmyo Masuno
Yokohama, Japan
www.kenkohji.jp/s
Photos: Minao Tabata

We all need time and distance to escape the rhythm of city life in order to rediscover nature and ourselves. Shunmyo Masuno leads the tenants of this residential building away from the noise of the streets through three artistic gates to a tranquil garden, the sound of flowing water and the feeling of warm stones.

Der Mensch benötigt Zeit und Distanz, um vom Rhythmus des Stadtlebens wieder zu dem der Natur und zu sich selbst zu finden. Shunmyo Masuno leitet die Bewohner dieses Wohngebäudes vom Straßenlärm weg durch drei stilisierte Tore in einen ruhigen Garten, zum Ton rinnenden Wassers und dem Gefühl von warmen Steinen.

L'homme a besoin de temps et de distance pour retourner à la nature et se retrouver, loin du rythme de la vie citadine. Shunmyo Masuno guide les occupants de cet immeuble résidentiel hors de portée du bruit des rues à travers trois portes stylisées, vers un jardin paisible, vers le son de l'eau qui coule et la sensation des pierres chaudes.

El ser humano requiere tiempo y cierta distancia para abandonar el ritmo urbano, regresar al de la naturaleza y reencontrarse consigo mismo. A través de tres estilizadas puertas de un plácido jardín, Shunmyo Masuno desvía a los habitantes del edificio del mundanal ruido y los traslada al fluir del agua y al calor de las piedras.

L'uomo ha bisogno di tempo e di distanza per poter ritrovare la natura e sé stesso, lontano dal ritmo della vita cittadina. Attraverso tre portoni stilizzati, Shunmyo Masuno conduce gli abitanti di questo caseggiato via dal rumore delle strade, in un giardino tranquillo, verso il suono dell'acqua che scorre e la sensazione di pietre calde.

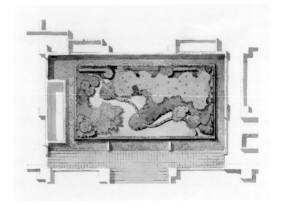

Rifugio

Okoyama Prefecture I Japan

Landscape architecture: Shunmyo Masuno
Yokohama, Japan
www.kenkohji.jp/s
Photos: Minao Tabata

The contractor wanted this garden to be a space "in which merely a hint of sun rays would make nature feel *tangible* to an observer inside. Even minute space can symbolize the myriad of the great world". It took philosophical serenity and joviality to turn this demand into reality.

Der Auftraggeber wünschte diesen Garten als Raum, „in dem nur durch einen Wink der Sonnenstrahlen dem Betrachter drinnen Natur *fühlbar* gemacht wird. Sogar ein winziger Raum kann die grenzenlose Welt vermitteln." Mit philosophischer Ruhe und Heiterkeit wurde diese Herausforderung meisterlich umgesetzt.

Le client voulait que son jardin soit un espace où « avec un soupçon de rayon de soleil, l'observateur *ressente* la nature à l'intérieur. Même un petit espace évoque l'infini du monde ». Ce défi a été brillamment relevé avec une paix et une sérénité philosophique.

El cliente que encargó este jardín quería un espacio "en el que con unos pocos rayos de sol se pudiera *sentir* la naturaleza en el interior. Hasta un espacio diminuto es capaz de transmitir la inmensidad del mundo". El reto se resolvió de forma magistral con serenidad filosófica y dinamismo.

Il committente desiderava che questo giardino fosse uno spazio "nel quale, anche solo quando il sole vi fa capolino, si possa far *percepire* la natura all'osservatore al suo interno. Persino uno spazio minuscolo può dare la sensazione dell'immensità del mondo". Tale compito è stato realizzato in modo esemplare, con pace e serenità filosofica.

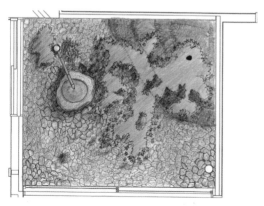

Nagoya Central Garden Residence

Nagoya I Japan

Architecture: Mitsubishi Jisho Sekkei, Inc.
Tokyo, Japan
www.mj-sekkei.com

Lighting plays an important role in the garden of this luxurious residential complex in the neighborhood of the Kakuoozan district. This is true of both the stone garden kept in light hues and the deeply dark-blue lake with waterproof lamps twinkling on it like stars in the sky.

Im Garten der luxuriösen Wohnanlage in Nachbarschaft des Kakuoozanviertels spielt die Beleuchtung eine wichtige Rolle. Das gilt sowohl für den in hellen Tönen gehaltenen Steingarten als auch für den tief dunkelblauen See, auf dem wie Sterne am Himmel wasserdichte Lampen funkeln.

Dans le jardin de ce luxueux complexe résidentiel près du quartier de Kakuoozan, l'éclairage joue un rôle important, à la fois pour le jardin de pierre dans des teintes claires et pour le lac bleu sombre sur lequel des lampes étanches brillent comme des étoiles dans le ciel.

En el jardín de este lujoso bloque de apartamentos cercano al barrio de Kakuoozan la iluminación desempeña un papel primordial, que se manifiesta, no sólo en el jardín de piedras de tonos claros, sino también en el oscuro estanque azul, en el que unas luminarias sumergibles resplandecen como estrellas en el firmamento.

Nel giardino della zona residenziale di lusso situata nelle vicinanze del quartiere Kakuoozan l'illuminazione ha un ruolo importante. Ciò vale sia per il giardino di rocce in tonalità chiare, sia per il lago blu intenso, nel quale brillano come stelle nel cielo le lampade impermeabili.

Cabbagetown Garden

Toronto I Canada

Landscape architecture: PLANT Architect Inc.
Toronto, Canada
www.branchplant.com
Photos: Peter Legris, Chris Pommer

Like a bridge, the aluminum stairs span this sea of ornamental plants that cover the majority of this narrow sloping garden. A new dining area in front of a unique wall made of stones left over from the renovation enhances the living space. New fences maintain intimacy.

Wie eine Brücke überquert die Aluminiumtreppe das Meer ornamentaler Pflanzen, die sich über den Großteil dieses schmalen Hanggartens ziehen. Eine neue Essecke vor einer originellen Wand aus von der Renovierung übriggebliebenen Steinen vergrößert die Wohnfläche, neue Zäune wahren die Intimität.

Comme un pont, les escaliers d'aluminium traversent l'océan de plantes ornementales qui s'étend sur la plus grande partie de cet étroit jardin en pente légère. Devant un mur original fait des pierres restant après la rénovation, un coin repas élargit l'espace de vie. Les nouvelles clôtures préservent l'intimité.

La escalera de aluminio atraviesa como un puente el mar de plantas ornamentales que se extiende por la mayor parte de este apretado jardín en pendiente. El comedor al aire libre ante un muro construido con las piedras sobrantes de la restauración, amplía la superficie habitable, y un vallado nuevo aporta intimidad.

I gradini in alluminio attraversano come un ponte il mare di piante ornamentali che ricopre la maggior parte di questo stretto giardino in pendenza. La superficie abitabile è ampliata da una nuova zona pranzo posta di fronte ad un originale muro di mattoni rimasti dalla ristrutturazione, mentre le nuove recinzioni preservano l'intimità.

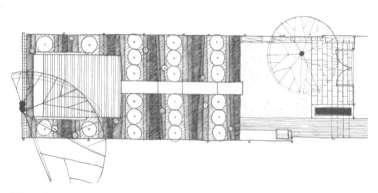

Roxborough Garden One

Toronto I Canada

Landscape architecture: PLANT Architect Inc.
Toronto, Canada
www.branchplant.com
Photos: Peter Legris

This small garden behind a traditional three-story town house stands out because of its large shady treetops. New plantings at medium height and covering the ground draw attention to different levels, down the shiny staircase and through the window frame into the adjacent park.

Dieser kleine Garten hinter einem traditionellen dreistöckigen Stadthaus besticht durch die schatten-spendenden großen Baumkronen. Neupflanzungen in mittlerer und Bodenhöhe lenken die Blicke auf verschiedene Ebenen, über die glänzende Treppe in die Tiefe und durch den Fensterrahmen in den angrenzenden Park.

Ce petit jardin derrière une maison de ville traditionnelle de trois étages séduit par l'ombre de son abondante frondaison. De nouvelles plantations, de taille moyenne et à ras de terre, dirigent le regard sur les différents niveaux, par-dessus l'escalier brillant, vers le bas du jardin et à travers le cadre de fenêtre, vers le parc attenant.

Este reducido jardín a espaldas de una tradicional vivienda urbana de tres plantas seduce por la sombra que brindan las grandes copas de sus árboles. Las nuevas plantas, a media altura y a ras de suelo, dirigen la mirada por los diferentes niveles, hacia el fondo atravesando la resplandeciente escalera y hacia el parque a través de los marco de las ventana.

Questo piccolo giardino posto sul retro di una tradizionale casa di città a tre piani è reso affascinante dalle grandi chiome ombrose degli alberi. Condottovi dalle nuove piante di bassa e media altezza, lo sguardo si posa su diversi livelli, verso il basso giù per i lucenti scalini e nel parco confinante attraverso le finestre.

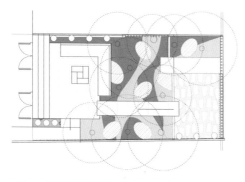

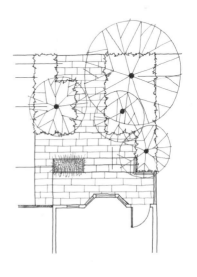

Artificial Reflections

Lombardy I Italy

Landscape architecture: Patrizia Pozzi with Fantini Mosaici (mosaic and marble),
Hydroware (green realizations), Salix (salix furniture)
Milan, Italy
www.patriziapozzi.it
Photos: Dario Fusaro, Patrizia Pozzi

The redesign of the garden merged the previously heterogeneous planted areas, paths and buildings into one overall unit. The ironic juxtaposition to the highly artistic flower mosaics of Carrara marble, river pebbles and Monte Spluga rocks on the paths is formed by the two sofas of artificial box tree behind the swimming pool.

Die Neugestaltung des Gartens fügte die zuvor heterogenen Grünflächen, Wege und Gebäude zu einem Gesamtwerk zusammen. Ironischen Kontrapunkt zu den kunstvollen Blumenmosaiken aus Carrara-Marmor, Flusskieseln und Steinen des Monte Spluga auf den Wegen sind die beiden Sofas aus Kunst-Buchsbaum hinter dem Schwimmbad.

Ce jardin a été redessiné pour rassembler les espaces verts, allées et bâtiments auparavant hétérogènes et constituer une œuvre globale. Les deux canapés de buis artificiel derrière la piscine forment le contrepoint ironique aux mosaïques de fleurs très artistiques en marbre de Carrare, au gravier de rivière et aux pierres de Monte Spugla sur les allées.

El objeto de la nueva composición de este jardín fue crear una obra unificada a partir de las zonas verdes, caminos y edificios dispuestos de forma heterogénea. El contrapunto irónico a los artísticos mosaicos florales de mármol de Carrara de los senderos, los guijarros de río y las piedras del monte Spluga, lo marcan los dos sofás podados de boj detrás de la piscina.

La ristrutturazione del giardino ha unito le superfici verdi, le strade e gli edifici precedentemente eterogenei in un'unica opera. Contrappunto ironico rispetto agli artistici mosaici floreali di marmo di Carrara, ciottoli di fiume e sassi del Monte Spluga, che ricoprono i viottoli, sono i due sofà di bosso sintetico dietro alla piscina.

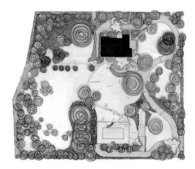

particolari della posa dei cubetti in pietra

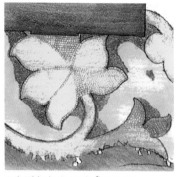

Cubetti in beola verde fiammata

Small Green Rooms

Bergamo I Italy

Landscape architecture: Patrizia Pozzi with Bettoni (building realizations),
Hydroware (green realizations), Salix (salix furniture)
Milan, Italy
www.patriziapozzi.it
Photos: Patrizia Pozzi

The garden design of a modernistic apartment plays with the positive-negative effects created by a vortex of gravel and grass. Aided by groups of camellias, it separates the private garden of the apartment from that of an ancient convent. The garden lights have been placed beneath spheres of willow reeds.

Die Gartengestaltung eines modernen Apartments spielt mit Positiv-Negativ-Effekten eines Wirbel-musters aus Splitt und Gras, und grenzt so, unterstützt von Kameliengruppen, den Privatgarten vom angrenzenden Garten eines alten Konvents ab. Die Gartenbeleuchtung befindet sich unter Kugeln aus Weidengeflecht.

La conception de ce jardin d'un appartement moderne joue avec les effets positif-négatif créés par des boucles de gravier et d'herbe. Agrémentées de massifs de camélias, elles créent une frontière entre le jardin privé et celui de l'ancien couvent voisin. L'éclairage du jardin est logé dans des boules d'osier tressé.

La configuración del jardín de una moderna vivienda juega con los efectos positivo y negativo de una espiral de grava y césped que, junto a unos grupos de camelias, separan el jardín privado del jardín perteneciente a un antiguo convento. La iluminación se esconde en unas esferas de mimbre.

Questo progetto del giardino di un appartamento moderno gioca con l'effetto positivo-negativo di un disegno a volute composto da erba e brecciolino, delimitando così, insieme a gruppi di camelie, il giardino privato dal giardino confinante di un antico convento. Le luci del giardino si trovano all'interno di sfere di vimini.

Cool Contemporary Classic

London I UK

Garden design: Charlotte Rowe
London, UK
www.charlotterowe.com
Photos: Charlotte Rowe Garden Design and Light IQ

The long rill is the eye-catcher of this city garden. Two cedar pontoons span its limestone paving. Shrubs and perennials are planted in a rhythmic pattern along its edge. Three multi-stemmed *Amelanchier lamarckii* and pleached *Carpinus betulus* draw one's eye upwards.

Der lange Kanal ist der Blickfang dieses Stadtgartens. Seine Einfassung aus Kalkstein wird von zwei Zedernholzstegen überquert. An der Seite wachsen Stauden und Büsche in rhythmischer Anordnung. Drei mehrstämmige *Amelanchier lamarckii* und verflochtene *Carpinus betulus* lenken den Blick in die Höhe.

Le long ruisseau est l'attraction principale de ce jardin de ville. Ses pavés en calcaire sont traversés par deux pontons de cèdre. Sur le côté, des arbustes et des plantes vivaces sont plantés dans une composition rythmique. Trois *Amelanchier lamarckii* touffus et des *Carpinus betulus* entrelacés dirigent le regard vers le haut.

El largo canal es principalmente lo que atrae la mirada en este jardín urbano. Dos pontones de cedro se extienden por el pavimento de piedra caliza, a los lados se ordenan rítmicamente los arbustos y las matas perennes. Tres *Amelanchier lamarckii* de varios troncos y unos *Carpinus betulus* entrelazados dirigen la mirada hacia lo alto.

Il lungo ruscello è ciò che attrae maggiormente lo sguardo in questo giardino di città. La sua pavimentazione in pietra calcarea è attraversata da due galleggianti pavimentati in legno di cedro. Gli arbusti e le piante perenni crescono lungo i bordi in ordine ritmico. I tre *Amelanchier lamarckii* a più rami e i *Carpinus betulus* intrecciati attirano lo sguardo verso l'alto.

Roof Terrace in Holland Park

London I UK

Garden design: Charlotte Rowe
London, UK
www.charlotterowe.com
Photos: Light IQ

The final touch to this roof terrace with its timber deck, interspersed with glass chippings, is the dramatic lighting. Perennial plants in containers provide a focus of color and the timber benches set between softly swaying grasses underline the real concept behind the garden—entertaining friends.

Das i-Tüpfelchen dieser Dachterrasse mit einem Boden aus Holz und Glassplit ist die dramatische Beleuchtung. Mehrjährige Pflanzen in Containern setzen Farbakzente und die Sitzgelegenheiten aus Holz zwischen den weich wogenden Gräsern weisen auf den eigentlichen Zweck des Gartens hin: den Empfang von Freunden.

L'éclairage spectaculaire est la touche finale de ce toiture terrasse au sol de bois constellé de verre. Des plantes vivaces en pot viennent mettre des touches de couleur, et les bancs de bois entre les graminées qui ondulent doucement révèlent le véritable concept se cachant derrière ce jardin : tout simplement recevoir des amis.

El toque de distinción de esta terraza en una azotea con tarima de madera y gravilla de cristal es la refinada iluminación. Especies de hoja perenne en maceteros le dan la pincelada de color. Los bancos de madera ubicados entre las gramíneas ligeramente combadas subrayan el verdadero objeto de este jardín: divertirse con los amigos.

Il tocco di classe di questa terrazza sul tetto con pavimento di legno, cosparso di vetro frantumato, è l'illuminazione drammatica. Le piante perenni nei contenitori donano note di colore e le banchine di legno posizionate tra l'erba leggermente ondeggiante sottolineano il concetto reale che c'è dietro al giardino: intrattenere gli amici.

PRIVATE SPACES . Roof Terrace in Holland Park

Duplex Sea Facing Apartment

Mumbai I India

Architecture: Rajiv Saini
Mumbai, India
www.rajivsaini.com
Photos: Sebastian Zachariah

Size doesn't matter that much after all. The design of these balconies with their views of the ocean and their plants is defined by the minimalist style. In sync with the markings on the stone and timber floors, the leaves of the plants in the indentations or containers change into graphic structures themselves.

Auf die Größe kommt es eben doch nicht immer an. Die Gestaltung dieser Balkone mit Meerblick und ihre Bepflanzung sind in einem reduzierten Stil gehalten. Abgestimmt auf die Zeichnung der Stein- und Holzböden werden die Blätter der Pflanzen in den Rillen oder Containern selbst zu grafischen Strukturen.

Après tout, ce n'est pas toujours la taille qui compte. L'architecture de ces balcons avec vue sur l'océan et leurs plantations gardent un style minimaliste. Coordonnées avec les marques sur les sols en pierre et en bois, les feuilles des plantes qui poussent dans les rainures ou dans les pots deviennent elles-mêmes des structures graphiques.

Ya no se trata de una cuestión de tamaño. La configuración de este balcón con sus plantas y vistas al mar ha seguido un estilo de reducidas dimensiones. En concordancia con el diseño del pavimento de piedra y madera, las hojas de las plantas en las zanjas y los maceteros conforman en sí estructuras gráficas.

La dimensione non è sempre la cosa più importante. Il progetto di questi balconi con vista sul mare e delle piante utilizzate adotta uno stile ridotto all'essenziale. In armonia con il disegno dei pavimenti in pietra e in legno, le foglie delle piante messe a dimora nei solchi del pavimento e nei contenitori diventano esse stesse delle strutture grafiche.

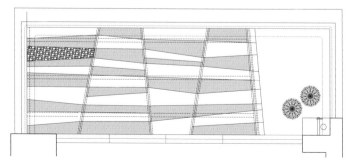

Caron

Campina Grande I Brazil

Landscape architecture: Slomp Busarello
Curitiba, Brazil
www.slompbusarello.com.br
Photos: Orlando Busarello

The designers of this garden played with light and shadows, colors and forms. Regional granite cut into even or uneven shapes appears both in the house and outside, organizing the paths, water surfaces and plant sculptures, which include royal palms, box tree, gardenias and others.

Die Gestalter dieses Gartens spielen mit Licht und Schatten, Farben und Formen. Regelmäßig oder unregelmäßig geschnittener regionaler Granit kommt sowohl im Haus als auch draußen zum Einsatz und organisiert die Wege, Wasserflächen und Pflanzenskulpturen: u.a. Königspalmen, Buchsbaum, Gardenien.

Les concepteurs de ce jardin jouent avec la lumière et les ombres, les couleurs et les formes. Le granit de la région, taillé de manière régulière ou irrégulière, est utilisé à la fois dans la maison et à l'extérieur, et organise les allées, les surfaces aquatiques et les sculptures végétales formées de palmiers royaux, de buis et de gardénias.

Los diseñadores de este jardín han jugado con la luz y las sombras, los colores y las formas. Granito de la región, cortado en formas regulares e irregulares, se ha integrado tanto en la casa como en el exterior, demarcando sendas, espacios con agua o esculturas vegetales con palmeras imperiales, boj o gardenias.

Gli ideatori di questo giardino giocano con la luce e l'ombra, con i colori e le forme. Il granito della regione, tagliato in modo regolare o irregolare, viene adoperato sia in casa che all'esterno e dà assetto alle strade, agli specchi d'acqua e alle piante scolpite, tra cui le palme reali, il bosso e le gardenie.

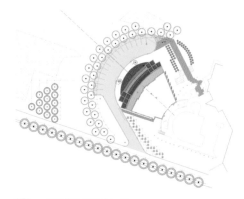

Simoes

Curitiba I Brazil

Landscape architecture: Slomp Busarello
Curitiba, Brazil
www.slompbusarello.com.br
Photos: Vilma Slomp, Orlando Busarello

Imagine a garden as the welcome bid of an art collector. Horizontal retaining walls of travertine create terraces at the slightly sloping site and equally clear and minimalist shapes form the framework for the swimming pool. The conifers around the edge take center stage in this spectacle of nature.

Ein Garten als Willkommensgruß eines Kunstsammlers. Horizontale Stützmauern aus Travertin terrassieren das leicht abfallende Gelände, und ebensolche klare, minimalistische Formen bilden den Rahmen für den Swimming Pool. In diesem Naturspektakel spielen die verschiedenfarbigen Koniferen am Rand die Hauptrolle.

Un jardin en guise de bienvenue d'un collectionneur d'art. Des murs de soutènement horizontaux en travertin créent des terrasses sur le terrain légèrement pentu. Des formes tout aussi claires et minimalistes forment le cadre de la piscine. Les conifères tout autour jouent un rôle majeur dans le spectacle de la nature.

Un jardín a modo de bienvenida de un coleccionista de arte. Los muros de contención horizontales de mármol travertino estructuran terrazas sobre el terreno en ligera pendiente. La piscina está enmarcada por formas claras y minimalistas semejantes. En este espectáculo natural, las multicolores coníferas de los márgenes son las protagonistas.

Un giardino come saluto di benvenuto di un collezionista d'arte. Le mura di sostegno orizzontali in travertino terrazzano il terreno leggermente in discesa, e forme altrettanto chiare e minimalistiche creano la cornice per la piscina. In questo spettacolo della natura rivestono il ruolo principale le conifere in diversi colori situate ai bordi.

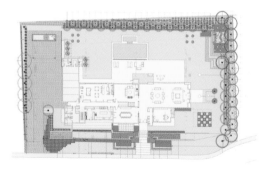

House 1

Barcelona I Spain

Architecture: Tonet Sunyer
Landscape architecture: Tonet Sunyer, Magda Sunyer
Barcelona, Spain
Photos: Magda Sunyer

Mediterranean plants like *Quercus suber* and *Phoenix canariensis* thrive easily with regard to pests and water consumption, ensuring sustainability. A spherical moon lamp hangs from one of the small-leafed trees (*Parkonsonia aculeata*) providing shade for the dining table.

Mediterrane Pflanzen wie *Quercus suber* und *Phoenix canariensis* gedeihen problemlos im Hinblick auf Schädlinge und Wasserverbrauch, sodass die Nachhaltigkeit gewahrt wird. In einem der kleinblättrigen Bäume (*Parkonsonia aculeata*), die den Esstisch beschatten, hängt eine kugelförmige Mond-Lampe.

Le développement durable du jardin est assuré par des plantes méditerranéennes comme le *Quercus suber* et le *Phoenix canariensis* qui prospèrent facilement car elles sont résistantes aux nuisibles et consomment peu d'eau. Une lampe ronde comme la lune est suspendue dans l'un des arbres aux petites feuilles (*Parkonsonia aculeata*) qui donnent leur ombre à la table.

Plantas mediterráneas como el *Quercus suber* o el *Phoenix canariensis* crecen sin excesivos problemas parasitarios o de consumo hídrico, con lo que su supervivencia está garantizada. En uno de los árboles de hojas diminutas (*Parkinsonia aculeata*), que da sombra a una mesa cuelga una lámpara esférica.

Piante mediterranee come la *Quercus suber* e la *Phoenix canariensis* crescono senza problemi relativi ai parassiti e al consumo d'acqua, così da garantire la sostenibilità. In uno degli alberi a foglia stretta (*Parkinsonia aculeata*) che donano ombra al tavolo da pranzo è stata appesa una lampada a forma di sfera.

Garden of Ghosts

Sydney I Australia

Landscape architecture: Vladimir Sitta (Terragram)
Surry Hills, Australia
www.terragram.com.au
Photos: Vladimir Sitta, Anthony Charlesworth

Elements of an old private zoo have been integrated into the design: doors, ladders and wall fragments. The raising of the pool and the planted border fulfill the safety regulations. A genuine aquarium wasn't feasible due to the stable water temperature it would have required, so a preserved specimen was exhibited in its place.

Teile des alten Privatzoos wurden in das Design einbezogen: Türen, Leitern, Mauerfragmente. Die Erhöhung des Pools und der bepflanzte Rand erfüllen die Sicherheitsvorschriften. Ein echtes Aquarium konnte aufgrund der nötigen konstanten Wassertemperatur nicht realisiert werden und wurde durch das Präparat ersetzt.

Des éléments de l'ancien zoo privé, portes, échelles et fragments de murs, ont été intégrés au design. Le rehaussement du bassin et la bordure de plantes répondent aux règles de sécurité. Il n'a pas été possible d'installer un véritable aquarium parce qu'il aurait fallu garder l'eau à une température constante. Cet animal naturalisé l'a donc remplacé.

En el diseño se incluyeron elementos el antiguo zoo privado tales como puertas, escaleras y fragmentos de muro. La elevación de la piscina y la vegetación circundante cumplen con la normativa de seguridad. A causa de los constantes cambios de temperatura no fue posible incluir un acuario real por lo que se sustituyó por un preparado.

Alcune parti del vecchio zoo privato sono state inglobate nel design: porte, scale, frammenti di muri. Innalzando la piscina e il bordo con le piante sono state rispettate le norme di sicurezza. Essendo necessaria una temperatura costante dell'acqua, non è stato possibile realizzare un vero acquario, al cui posto c'è un esemplare preservato in formalina.

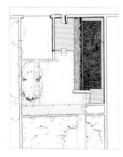

Red Garden

Sydney I Australia

Landscape architecture: Vladimir Sitta (Terragram)
Surry Hills, Australia
www.terragram.com.au
Photos: Vladimir Sitta, Anthony Charlesworth

What's very striking here are the corners of the red sandstone wall that look different from every angle. Some of the succulents come from the garden owner's collection while others were added. Growing slowly in a special mix of gravel substrate, they're going to undergo a fascinating shift in colors.

Sehr markant sind die Mauerecken aus rotem Sandstein, die aus jedem Blickwinkel anders aussehen. Einige der Sukkulenten stammen aus der Sammlung des Gartenbesitzers, andere wurden hinzugefügt. Langsam in speziell gemischtem Kiessubstrat wachsend werden sie eine spannende Farbverschiebung vornehmen.

Les coins de murs en grès rouge qui paraissent changer, vus sous un angle différent, sont particulièrement remarquables. Certaines des plantes grasses proviennent de la propre collection du propriétaire du jardin, d'autres ont été rajoutées. Elles offriront un agencement de couleurs captivant en poussant lentement dans leur substrat mêlé de gravier, fabriqué spécialement à cet usage.

Las esquinas de los muros en arenisca roja con formas cambiantes según la perspectiva crean un marcado relieve. Algunas de las crasuláceas proceden de la colección del propietario del jardín; otras se añadieron posteriormente. Sobre un sustrato de grava mezclado ex profeso, van creciendo y adquiriendo espectaculares tonalidades cromáticas.

Colpiscono senz'altro l'attenzione gli angoli dei muri in pietra arenaria rossa, che appaiono diversi da ogni prospettiva. Alcune delle piante grasse vengono dalla collezione del proprietario, altre sono state aggiunte. Crescendo lentamente in uno speciale substrato di ghiaia mista, esibiscono un'interessante alternanza di colori.

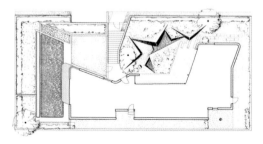

Beverly Hills Pool House

Beverly Hills I California, USA

Architecture: Tichenor & Thorp Architects
Beverly Hills, California, USA
www.tichenorandthorp.com
Photos: Brian Tichenor

A grass carpet frames the modern architecture of the new pool house with its almost panorama-like view and the swimming pool. Aloe plants, Fountain Grass and Mexican feather grass catch the eye even as they endure dry spells without any need for special care.

Die moderne Architektur des neuen Poolhauses mit beinahe Rundumblick und der Swimming Pool werden von einem Teppich aus Gras eingerahmt. Aloe-Pflanzen, rotes Lampenputzergras sowie mexikanisches Federgras sind Blickfänge, obwohl sie anspruchslos sind und Trockenperioden überstehen.

L'architecture moderne du nouveau bâtiment de la piscine, qui offre une vue extrêment dégagée, et la piscine elle-même sont entourées d'un tapis de pelouse. Des aloès, des *pennisetum* rouges et des *Stipa tenuissima* en sont les attractions principales, même si ces plantes ne nécessitent aucun entretien particulier et peuvent supporter des périodes sèches.

La moderna arquitectura de la nueva casita de la piscina, levantada frente a una panorámica de casi 360°, y la propia piscina están enmarcadas en una alfombra de hierba. Plantas de aloe, panizo chino rojo y cerrillo mexicano constituyen un punto de atención, aun cuando no requieren cuidado especial y sobreviven a los periodos secos.

Un tappeto d'erba incornicia la piscina ed il nuovo fabbricato adiacente dall'architettura moderna, con vista quasi a 360 gradi. Le piante di aloe, penniseto allungato e *Stipa tenuissima* attirano l'attenzione, sebbene non richiedano molta cura, e sopravvivono ai periodi di siccità.

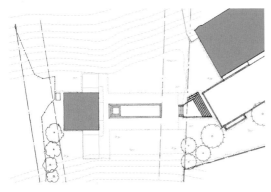

Cielo e Mare

Southern California I California, USA

Architecture: Tichenor & Thorp Architects
Beverly Hills, California, USA
www.tichenorandthorp.com
Photos: Brian Tichenor

Three areas distinguish this effective garden. Succulents survive well in the salty air of Pacific Coast, while flowering bougainvillea, aloes, *sedum* (stonecrops), *arctotis* (African daisies) and rosemary create a Mediterranean flair at the center. All the way above, palms and New Zealand metrosidero trees offer protection from the sun as well as privacy.

Drei Bereiche zeichnen diesen effektvollen Garten aus. Sukkulenten vertragen die salzige Luft an der Pazifikküste gut, während blühende Bougainvillea, Aloes, Fetthenne, Arctotis und Rosmarin in der Mitte Mittelmeerflair schaffen. Ganz oben bieten Palmen und Eisenholzbäume Sonnen- und Sichtschutz.

Trois zones distinguent ce jardin qui fait beaucoup d'effets. Les plantes grasses supportent bien l'air salé de la Côte Pacifique, et les bougainvillées, les aloès, les *sedum*, les *arctotis* et le romarin en fleurs créent une touche méditerranéenne au centre. Tout en haut, les palmiers et les metrosideros néozélandais assurent une protection contre le soleil et garantissent l'intimité.

Tres áreas definen este jardín efectista. Las plantas crasuláceas que toleran el salitre del aire de la costa del Pacífico; buganvillas, aloes, sedum, arctotis y romero dando un aire mediterráneo a la zona central; y en la parte más alta, palmeras y árboles de hierro protegen del sol y de miradas indiscretas.

Tre aree contraddistinguono questo giardino di sicuro effetto. Le piante grasse sopportano bene l'aria salmastra delle coste del Pacifico, mentre la buganvillea in fiore, l'aloe, il sedo, l'arctotis e il rosmarino creano al centro una nota mediterranea. In cima le palme e i metrosideros della Nuova Zelanda offrono protezione dal sole e dagli sguardi indiscreti.

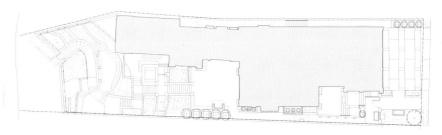

Taj Wellington Mews

Mumbai I India

Architecture: John Portman and Associates
USA – www.portmanusa.com
Landscape architecture: P.T. Wijaya (Made Wijaya)
Sanur, Bali, Indonesia – www.ptwijaya.com
Photos: Made Wijaya, courtesy Taj Hotels

Easy-care tropical plants, 10-feet tall walls adorned with art and a trick fountain in the shape of a hill decorate this modern housing complex. A jogging path in a triple helix frames the elliptical lawns. The surrounding trees give a park-like character to this rooftop garden.

Pflegeleichte tropische Pflanzen, drei Meter hohe künstlerisch verzierte Wände sowie ein Wasserspiel in Hügelform dekorieren die moderne Wohnanlage. Ein Joggingpfad in dreifacher Helix rahmt die elliptischen Rasenflächen. Der umgebende Baumbestand verleiht der Anlage, die ein Dachgarten ist, Parkcharakter.

Des plantes tropicales faciles d'entretien, des murs de trois mètres de haut décorés avec art et un jeu d'eau en forme de colline agrémentent ce complexe résidentiel moderne. La triple hélice du parcours de jogging encadre les pelouses en forme d'ellipse. Les arbres environnants font ressembler le complexe, qui est en fait une toiture terrasse, à un parc.

El moderno complejo residencial se ha decorado con plantas tropicales de fácil cuidado, paredes de tres metros con artísticos motivos y una fuente semiesférica. Un sendero para practicar *footing* de triple espiral enmarca la superficie de césped elíptica. La arboleda circundante confiere carácter de parque a esta azotea-jardín.

Questo moderno complesso residenziale è abbellito da piante tropicali facili da curare, muri alti tre metri decorati da artisti e un gioco d'acqua a forma di cupola. Un percorso jogging a forma di triplice elica incornicia le zone erbose ellittiche. Gli alberi circostanti conferiscono al giardino, posto su un tetto, l'aspetto di un parco.

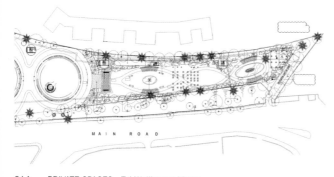

MAIN ROAD

Vijoo

Bangalore I India

Architecture: Sandeep Khosla
Bangalore, India – www.khoslaassociates.com
Landscape architecture: P.T. Wijaya (Made Wijaya)
Sanur, Bali, Indonesia – www.ptwijaya.com
Photos: Made Wijaya

In close coordination with new star architect Sandeep Khosla, the courtyards of this residential building were designed with only few accents: Old stone slabs for the floor, modern shiny plant pots, a wall mosaic by Bombay artist Chiru and a free-standing sculpture by Made Cangker of Bali.

In enger Abstimmung mit dem neuen Stararchitekten Sandeep Khosla wurden die Gartenhöfe dieses Wohnhauses mit wenigen Akzenten gestaltet: Alte Steinplatten für den Boden, moderne glänzende Pflanztöpfe, ein Wandmosaik vom Bombayer Künstler Chiru und eine freistehende Skulptur von Made Cangker aus Bali.

En étroite collaboration avec le nouvel architecte star Sandeep Khosla, on a conçu les cours jardins de cet immeuble résidentiel avec peu de détails : de vieilles dalles de pierre pour le sol, des pots de plantes modernes et brillants, une mosaïque murale de l'artiste Chiru, originaire de Bombay, et une sculpture libre du Balinais Made Cangker.

De mutuo acuerdo con Sandeep Khosla, nuevo arquitecto de élite, se optó por no recargar los patios ajardinados de esta residencia: antiguas planchas de piedra como pavimento, modernos y resplandecientes maceteros, mosaicos murales de Chiru, el artista de Bombay, y una escultura del balinés Made Cangker.

In perfetto accordo con il nuovo architetto di successo Sandeep Khosla i cortili verdi di questa casa sono stati allestiti con pochi elementi: vecchie lastre di pietra per il pavimento, vasi lucidi e moderni per le piante, un mosaico a muro dell'artista di Bombay Chiru e una scultura autoportante eseguita da Made Cangker di Bali.

Other titles published in this series

Cool Hotels London
ISBN 978-3-8327-9206-0

Cool Hotels New York
ISBN 978-3-8327-9207-7

Cool Hotels Paris
ISBN 978-3-8327-9205-3

Cool Hotels Italy
ISBN 978-3-8327-9234-3

Cool Hotels Spain
ISBN 978-3-8327-9230-5

Cool Hotels Spa & Wellness
ISBN 978-3-8327-9243-5

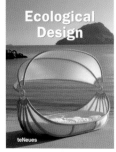

Ecological Design
ISBN 978-3-8327-9229-9

Ecological Houses
ISBN 978-3-8327-9227-5

Garden Design
ISBN 978-3-8327-9228-2